THE

Executor's Handbook

*A Practical Guide
to Settling
Connecticut Estates*

SECOND EDITION

Additional copies of this book may be ordered from:
Chase Publishing Company
88 Cherry Hill Road
Greenwich, CT 06831
or by telephing: 203-351-4248

Also by Gayle Brian Wilhelm

THE CONNECTICUT LIVING TRUST
Cornerstone of Modern Estate Planning

CONNECTICUT ESTATES PRACTICE
in seven volumes:

DEATH TAXES *Second Edition*
SETTLEMENT OF ESTATES
INCAPACITY AND ADOPTION *(with Folsom) Second Edition*
WILLS *(with Folsom)*
JURISDICTION *(with Folsom)*
TRUSTS *(with Folsom and Bourdeau)*
REVOCABLE TRUSTS

About the Authors

Gayle Brian Wilhelm is a senior partner of the Connecticut and Florida law firm of Cummings & Lockwood and a fellow of the American College of Trust and Estate Counsel. He is an honors graduate of Harvard College and the Harvard Law School, and concentrates his practice in the field of estate and trust planning, including estate settlement, trust management, taxation and litigation. Mr. Wilhelm's prior publications include the seven volume *Connecticut Estates Practice* legal treatise on estate settlement, taxation, wills and trusts and (with Emogene C. Wilhelm), *The Executor's Handbook – A Practical Guide to Settling Connecticut Estates, Second Edition.* He makes his home in Old Greenwich, Connecticut.

Emogene C. Wilhelm is a practicing attorney in Greenwich, Connecticut. She is an honors graduate of Simmons College and the University of Bridgeport School of Law where she was an editor of the *Law Review.* Mrs. Wilhelm is well known in the Connecticut educational community after serving for many years on the Greenwich Board of Education and on the Board of Cooperative Educational Services of Fairfield County.

THE
Executor's
Handbook

*A Practical Guide
to Settling
Connecticut Estates*

SECOND EDITION

Gayle Brian Wilhelm, Esq.
Emogene C. Wilhelm, Esq.

CHASE PUBLISHING COMPANY
Old Greenwich, Connecticut

NOTE

This volume is intended as a source of general information about estate settlement and various related subjects. It is not a legal reference, and no reader should rely for legal advice on any matters discussed in the text. Such matters should be discussed fully with an experienced estate attorney admitted to practice in Connecticut before any actions are taken.

Attorneys who wish to review a legal treatise on this subject, complete with suggested forms and annotations, may find such materials in Wilhelm & Folsom, *Connecticut Estates Practice – Settlement of Estates* (Lawyers Cooperative Publishing Company, Rochester, New York 1974).

Chase Publishing Company
Post Office Box 303
Old Greenwich, Connecticut 06870

ISBN 0-9637764-0-1

*This book is dedicated to
the probate judges of Connecticut
who are always available
for consultation and who do such a fine job
guiding families through
the most difficult period in their lives.*

Foreword to the Second Edition

If there is one common thread among the many estate planning clients estate and trust attorneys see each year, it is a belief that designation as executor is an honor—a privilege to be conferred magnanimously and accepted with pride. Yet we know from years of experience that settling the estate of a family member, a close friend or a business associate can be one of the most difficult, time-consuming, unpleasant and least rewarding experiences of a life-time. Why should this be so? And, why should the object of this dubious honor so often be the surviving spouse, when his or her initial reaction is likely to be one of concern, uncertainty, and sometimes horror over the nature of the obligations assumed?

We hope this book will shed light on the subject. In smaller and less complicated estates, there is often no reason to assume the expense of naming a professional executor, for with some guidance the surviving spouse or other family member can do the job. For those who use this book as a planning tool, we hope that our comments will be useful in helping you decide how much of the burden you can shoulder alone and when and in which areas you need professional help.

Estate settlement for a large or complicated estate, on the other hand, is a job for professionals. This does not mean the family has no part to play, only that the intricacies of tax laws and administrative regulations require professional guidance. While the legal profession and the banks are accustomed to shouldering most of the burdens of estate settlement, this tends to perpetuate the myth that estate settlement is, at the same time, both mysterious and not much trouble at all. This is because the family member is seldom asked to do anything and rarely understands what the professional is doing.

If you are a newly appointed executor who has chosen this book hoping that mysteries can be unveiled, or at least that you can understand what your attorney is recommending, then we think you will find the chapters which follow to be of great help. Every effort has been made to avoid legal fictions and cut through the thicket of tax and legal jargon in order to help you understand the steps which lie ahead of you.

This second edition of *The Executor's Handbook* is being published at the same time as *The Connecticut Living Trust – Cornerstone of Modern Estate Planning* by Gayle B. Wilhelm, which is available through Chase Publishing Company, Box 303, Old Greenwich, Connecticut 06870. Contrary to the public's perception, probate and avoiding probate are not incompatible approaches to estate planning; in almost all cases they comfortably co-exist. You and your estate-planning advisor should understand both and apply each where best suited to the needs of your family.

G. B. W.
E. C. W.

Contents

Foreword   *vii*

1. How an Executor is Chosen – Who, Why and How   1
2. Finding the Right Lawyer   5
3. How the Probate Court System Works   8
4. Avoiding Probate – Good, Bad or Indifferent?   11
5. Last Minute Tax and Other Planning Steps   14
6. Funeral Arrangements   20
7. Understanding the Will   22
8. Selecting Professional Assistance   26
9. The Executor's Duties – A Broad Outline   30
10. Probating the Will   36
11. Disputes over the Will   38
12. Family Rights and Allowances   42
13. Valuing Estate Assets   44
14. Preparing the Inventory of Estate Assets   47
15. Debts and Claims   49
16. Taxes   52
17. Costs of Estate Settlement: Executor's Commissions,
    Attorney's Fees, Court Costs, and Other Expenses   60
18. Estimating and Raising Cash Requirements   66
19. Distribution and Division of Estate Assets   68
20. Record Keeping   74

21. Investing Estate Assets   78
22. Selling Estate Assets   81
23. Out-of-State Assets   84
24. Collecting Insurance, Social Security, Other Benefits   88
25. Accountings   91
26. Guardians for Children   93
27. Small Estates – Special Procedures   94
28. Living Trusts – The Probate Alternative   96
29. Frequently Asked Questions   99
30. Some Non-Lawyerly Hints for the Widow or Widower   105 *104*

APPENDICES

A. Sample Probate Court Forms Used in Settling
   an Estate   109
B. Connecticut Succession Tax Table   137
C. Sample Cash Requirements and Distribution
   Memorandum   141
D. Bibliography and Other Useful Reading Material for
   the Executor   145
E. Federal Estate and Gift Tax Rates   146
F. Distribution of Property According to Connecticut
   Laws of Intestacy   147
G. Sample Probate Court Accounting   148
H. Glossary of Legal Terminology   157

BOOK ORDER FORMS   165

1

How an Executor Is Chosen –
Who, Why and How

This book begins with a problem you will encounter throughout the process of estate planning and estate settlement – recognizing, understanding, and learning to use the terminology of the legal profession. Fortunately, there is a limited number of entirely new words or expressions, many of which are explained in Appendix H. An easy place to begin is with the title, *executor*. An executor is the person selected to settle the affairs of a person who has died and to carry out the terms of his or her will. Strictly speaking, the term refers only to a per-son actually named in the decedent's will – for example:

> I appoint my wife, Sarah, as executor of my Will.
> If she cannot act, I appoint my daughter, Sally.

If there is no will or the named executor does not accept this responsibility, the court will appoint an appropriate person to settle the estate. Usually this is a close family member, but it can be a bank or an experienced professional. Such a person is called an administrator rather than an executor. The responsibilities of an executor and an administrator are much the same, except that the will often will grant an executor broader powers than our state statutes give to administrators.

What does an executor do, and why do we need one? Let's recognize at the outset that in the large majority of estates, usually small in size, the executor will be a member of the family, and very little will be required of him or her. More often than not, the attorney selected by the executor is willing to handle most of the executor's responsibilities. The executor's principal job, then, is to use good judgment in selecting a qualified attorney, and then review, approve, and sign the various court and tax documents.

As a person's affairs become more complicated by investments, business dealings, and otherwise, the executor's job likewise becomes more complicated. Eventually it can become one of the most difficult, time-consuming, and frustrating responsibilities of a lifetime – one usually calling for an experienced professional. Plainly it's important to know in advance whether a particular executor's duties are intended to be honorary or onerous, or a little of each. This knowledge is equally useful to the living person preparing to draw a will, who must choose an executor, and to the chosen executor who later must decide whether to accept the responsibility. How can you tell? There are no absolute rules, but certainly there are useful guidelines:

1. Will tax planning be necessary?

Significant tax planning may be required when the executor must prepare a federal estate tax return. Under present law, such a return is required where the value of the estate exceeds $600,000. For this purpose, the value of the estate includes insurance, employee pensions and other company benefits, one-half of property jointly owned with a spouse, and all solely owned investments, businesses, bank accounts, etc. A bank or other professional executor will know exactly how to prepare the tax returns so as to minimize taxes and liabilities.

2. *Is there any potential dispute over the disposition of the estate?*

Family quarrels are rare, but they do occur. An independent and experienced executor can be helpful.

3. *Do investments, business interests or tax considerations require special attention?*

If so, be sure to pick an executor with the necessary talents and experience, or at least one who has the judgment to hire good advisors.

4. *Will money management be a problem?*

Some estates require only that the executor hold onto family properties. Others demand careful analysis of investments, sale of some assets and purchase of others. Are there large amounts of cash, such as insurance proceeds to be invested? Does the family have the experience to do this?

These and other considerations should be discussed carefully with your attorney in advance of choosing an executor or accepting appointment as one. It may be useful to bear in mind that three common approaches to choice of executors are:

a. *Single family executor:* Most married persons designate their husbands or wives as executor, usually as sole executor where the spouse is financially experienced or the estate is small and uncomplicated. Alternatively, a child or other family member is used. While two or more family members can be used as co-executors, this can be cumbersome and should be avoided in the absence of good reasons.

b. *Family member with bank or other experienced professional executor as co-executors:* In larger estates which will benefit substantially from professional management, it is common to designate the surviving spouse (or other family member) as a co-executor along with a bank or other experienced professional. Here the thought is that the experienced executor will assume the day-to-day responsibilities of estate settlement, while the family representative participates in important decisions and insures that various family interests are not overlooked.

c. Sole professional executor: We noted earlier that the executor's job can be burdensome. Certainly it is a dubious honor to bestow upon a family member who has no particular interest or experience for the job – for example, a widow or widower who would rather be on the golf course than helping appraise securities. In such cases, the appointment of a bank, lawyer or other experienced professional as sole executor is recommended.

2

Finding the Right Lawyer

Often the first question asked by an executor is one of the most difficult to answer: "Do I need a lawyer?" Occasionally the answer is "no" where the estate is small in value. If in doubt, talk to your local probate judge and take his advice. If a lawyer is needed, finding the right lawyer is not always an easy task. Many estates can be handled competently by a general practitioner; others demand the attention of highly skilled probate specialists. Failure to exercise prudence in selecting a lawyer with the necessary qualifications can mean personal liability for the executor. It can also make your job much more difficult and unpleasant. In making the initial decision as to what level of professional skill is required, you will find it worthwhile to ask the following questions:

1. How large is the estate? It is a reliable rule of thumb that the larger the estate, the greater the tax and other benefits available through skilled professional assistance.

2. Did the decedent rely heavily on a particular attorney for assistance during lifetime? If so, do the skills of that attorney carry over to estate settlement? Or was the lifetime attorney a business specialist with no expertise in estate matters – or maybe just a good friend or golf buddy?

3. Is there a will? If so, the attorney who prepared that will usually has some familiarity with his or her client's business affairs and intentions in disposing of the estate.

4. What is the nature of the assets requiring estate administration? Do they require careful tax preparation? Do they require special business or legal skills?

5. How willing are you, as executor, to devote hundreds of hours to estate settlement? If you prefer to be involved mainly in a supervisory or monitoring capacity, will you need an attorney who has accountants and paralegals on his or her staff to take care of bookkeeping and other responsibilities of the executor?

In assessing the needs of the estate and the qualifications of attorneys, you should give thought to the legal charges you will incur. While the legal fees of an attorney for an executor are payable from the estate, and not by the executor personally, the executor has the responsibility to see to it that the estate receives good value. Frequently there is little difference between the charges of one attorney and another for estate settlement. If that proves to be true, you might just as well hire the best legal talent available.

Having made your basic decision as to the qualifications needed for representing the estate, where do you turn for assistance in finding the right lawyer – especially if you decide you need the assistance of a probate specialist? Since few of your friends will have had frequent contact with lawyers settling estates, your best bet is to seek the advice of other professionals who work in fields related to estate settlement. Your local bank, for example, probably will have a good working knowledge of the skills as well as the charges of lawyers in your community who handle estate settlement. Likewise, you could talk to accountants, insurance agents, financial planners, or lawyers who don't handle estate settlement work and are, therefore, likely to have an impartial view. You will probably find that the names of certain attorneys tend to appear on the referral lists of different types of professionals, and if so, you can feel reasonably confident that these are the attorneys who have a good reputation for quality service.

If the estate is complicated, a good source of information for you to consider is the membership roster of the American College of Trust and Estate Counsel. This is an extremely selective organization, in which fellowship can be obtained only through satisfaction of rigorous qualifications as a probate lawyer. Election to membership in the college is by written vote of existing members, thus insuring that fellows of the American College are those probate lawyers most respected by their peers. You can obtain information with respect to fellows of the college by calling the head of the trust and estates department of any large law firm.

Finally, consider a visit to your local library. Two publications can be useful. One, the *Martindale-Hubbell Law Directory,* has biographical and professional information about most practicing attorneys. The second, Naifeth and Smith's *The Best Lawyers in America*, contains a list (by state, town or city) of lawyers specializing in trust and estate matters. The selections were made by vote of other lawyers in the state, and appear reliable.

3

How the Probate Court System Works

Connecticut has a simple, economical, and prompt court system for settling estates. Each probate court generally serves one city or large town or a group of smaller towns. The judges are elected by the public and are responsive to the needs of families. In the case of estate settlement, there are only a few formal, required procedures – and these are very straightforward and uncomplicated:

1. The application for probate

An application is sent to the court, asking for approval of the decedent's will and confirmation of the executor's authority to act. This is a pre-printed one-page form, a large part of which is devoted to space for listing the names and addresses of heirs and beneficiaries. (See Appendix A, Form 1.)

2. The public hearing

The court first sends notices to persons interested in the estate. (See Appendix A, Form 2.) Then the court holds a hearing to determine the validity of the will and approve the named executor. This generally lasts only a few minutes and frequently is not attended by anyone other than the judge (except in the rare case of a contested will). After the executor is approved, the court will issue to the executor *Certificates of*

Appointment, which can be presented to banks, insurance companies, brokers, etc. to show the executor's authority to conduct estate business. (See Appendix A, Form 3.)

3. *The notice to creditors*

The clerk of the court publishes a newspaper notice alerting creditors of the decedent to present their bills to the executor. (See Appendix A, Form 4.) The executor may also choose to notify known creditors in writing in order to force them to submit their claims promptly.

4. *The inventory of estate assets*

The executor prepares and sends to the court an inventory (a list of the property owned by the decedent and its fair market value). (See Appendix A, Form 5.)

5. *The accounting*

After the estate is settled and all taxes paid, the executor prepares a final accounting. This is a report of what has happened to the decedent's property during settlement of the estate, such as payment of debts, payment of taxes, collection of income, sales and purchases of assets, distributions to the beneficiaries, etc. (See Appendix A, Form 6.) Prior to this proceeding, the executor also must give the court a list of all creditors' claims which have been presented and show whether they have been paid or rejected. (See Appendix A, Form 7.)

6. *The closing affidavit*

Finally, the executor files with the court a simple statement to the effect that all estate matters have been concluded, final distribution of estate assets has been made, and the estate is closed. (See Appendix A, Form 8.)

That's it! Doesn't sound too complicated, does it? Of course, in many estates, the property owned by the decedent can create unusual problems, and if so, the court is available to help the executor if he wants help. This help could include, where appropriate:

1. *Disputed claims:* If the executor isn't sure whether he or she should pay certain bills of the decedent or claims of any kind, the court can authorize either payment in full or a compromise with the creditor.

2. *Interpretation of the will:* The executor may be uncertain how to distribute estate assets or the proper interpretation of the will. As part of the accounting proceeding, he or she can set forth a proposed distribution and obtain court approval.

3. *Sale of property:* Various procedures are available to obtain court approval or assistance in establishing the method of sale, the sales price, or the terms of sale.

There is nothing mysterious about our court procedures for estate settlement. They are designed to assist, not hinder, the executors and the family. The entire judicial process can be over in a matter of a few months, and often is. Lengthy delays in settlement usually are related to tax problems, not probate problems. But that's another matter entirely. (See Chapter 16.)

4

Avoiding Probate –
Good, Bad or Indifferent?

In the preceding chapter we have discussed the Connecticut probate court system. By now you should understand that we have a simple, straightforward, and inexpensive system for handling the legal aspects of estate settlement. Today's probate court system is designed to protect surviving family members against the mishandling of estate matters, and for many people it would be unwise to forego that protection without sound reasons.

On the other hand, regardless of the good features of the probate court system, in large measure it is intended to serve multiple and sometimes competing interests. Connecticut law allows us to custom-design our own system for addressing the problems of settling estates, and one of those systems – the living trust – will be discussed in Chapter 28.

The probate court system has not always enjoyed a good reputation, however. In the 1960's, Norman F. Dacey's publication *How to Avoid Probate!* created a national furor and aroused the ire of a large segment of the legal community. A prominently displayed quotation from an article in the *American Bar Association Journal* did little to help – it described the system in Mr. Dacey's home state, Connecticut, as:

> ...one of the most viciously corrupt systems ever
> distorted by the inventive minds of the greedy.

Several lawsuits followed, including one in Connecticut, providing further publicity for the book and its suggested techniques. Avoiding probate duly became a *cause célèbre.*
The great oddity was that Mr. Dacey's *exposé* was years behind the times. By the mid-twentieth century, our various state probate systems had few of the objectionable traits celebrated in his book. What few bad apples existed were, for the most part, corrected during the 1960's; today there are few remnants of the old abuses.

Nonetheless, for many people the probate process still is an object of dark suspicion. Why this should be so undoubtedly relates to a general apprehension of death as well as to lack of public knowledge about the legal process known as "going through probate." The subject matter is shunned by a large segment of the population. Frequently, it is only as a result of the encouragement of professionals that estate planning is undertaken at all.

It is true that many attorneys publicly speak out on the advantages of estate planning, but they reach only a handful of the public. Life underwriters, financial planners and others have done an excellent job in promoting estate planning, but lacking a broad background of legal training, they are not as well equipped as attorneys to assess the relative merits of the probate system. Their lack of personal experience with the probate courts and the public's fear of going through probate have led inexorably to the marketing of avoiding probate as a principal focus of estate planning – and that's unfortunate.

The focus of estate planning should be on how best to accomplish family purposes such as financial management and protection against creditors, conserving the estate through long range tax planning, and selection of fiduciaries (executors, trustees and guardians) in those situations where the family needs outside help. Those who prey on the public's fears of probate seldom understand the real objectives of sound estate planning, and it would be amusing (were it not so sad) to subject to closer scrutiny many of the so-called "reasons for avoiding probate." Some which have been advanced include:

Exaggerated Claims	*Reality*
Avoiding probate keeps the family's affairs a secret	How many of us really have those kinds of secrets
Avoiding probate avoids court fees	Court fees are based on the value of the taxable estate, not the probate estate, and are exactly the same whether one avoids probate or not
Avoiding probate saves estate taxes	Not at all—there is absolutely no difference

Nonetheless, we should not allow the real issue to be obscured by our disagreement with those who use avoiding probate as a scare tactic to market their products and services. There can be sound reasons for avoiding probate, particularly for those persons who are confident that they have left the settlement of their estates in good hands and that therefore their families do not need the added protection and professionalism that our probate court judges give us.

5

Last Minute Tax
and Other Planning Steps

It's not uncommon to have some advance warning of death. A natural and practical reaction is to question whether there are steps that should be taken to ensure maximum financial protection for the surviving family, minimize the impact of taxes, reduce the costs of eventual estate settlement, or otherwise plan ahead. Frequently there are a number of things which can be done which will be of great benefit to the surviving family.

Some of the available steps require the cooperation of the person who is facing death, however, and an initial judgment must be made as to whether he or she is competent to participate in decision making. Even if so, the benefits to be derived from advance planning must be weighed against possible adverse psychological reactions. Often the terminally ill person will take an active interest in planning ahead, and indeed may derive a great deal of satisfaction from participating in this process. Yet close friends, business associates and particularly the husband or wife may reject professional help in order to shelter the terminally ill person from knowledge or constant reminders of the situation. If the decision is made to act, then listed below are some of the areas where advance planning can be most helpful.

14

1. Review the estate plan

This will be the last opportunity to ensure that the estate has been properly planned to conserve taxes and reduce expenses, and also to verify that there has been no change in family circumstances which would warrant basic changes in the will. If the attorney who will represent the estate is known, he or she should be consulted immediately for best results. The designated executor should be informed and encouraged to participate in the planning as well.

This is also a final opportunity to consider whether and to what extent a living trust can play a role in the overall estate plan. If a living trust already exists, all property interests should be reviewed to determine if they should be transferred into the name of the trustees of the living trust before death.

2. Review assets

Each asset which will be a part of the eventual estate or which will be in any manner affected by a death of the individual involved, should be carefully reviewed to determine that ownership and beneficiary designations are all in order. Some potential problem areas and suggestions are:

a. *Life insurance:* Assemble all insurance policies. Check the actual policies to find out who is the owner of the insurance and who is the beneficiary. Make sure the premiums are being paid as they are due. Check the settlement option. Have the estate attorney determine whether the insurance provisions are compatible with the basic estate plan.

b. *Company benefits:* If the individual is employed or has retired, check all available company benefits. Have the director of personnel (or other company official) prepare a complete list of benefits, indicating amounts involved, ownership, beneficiaries, and settlement options. Check the expected tax status of each benefit.

c. *Business interests:* Review any agreements among the stockholders. Discuss arrangements for keeping the business going with minimum interruption. How are inheritance taxes on the business going to be paid? Are any of the assets nominally owned by the company actually personal assets? If so, should title be transferred? Conversely, are there assets owned by the individual which should be a part of the business? Does the will leave the business to the right person?

d. *Bank accounts:* Check to make sure all bank accounts are correctly registered. If they are in joint names and will pass to the other-named owner at death, is this consistent with the intent of all concerned? Are there bank accounts in another state which will be frozen at death, but which can be moved before death to avoid that result?

e. *Stocks and bonds:* Are there securities which should be sold before death for tax advantages or administrative convenience? Are there securities which should *not* be sold? Are brokerage accounts registered in the proper name? Are the securities themselves registered in the proper name? If any securities are owned jointly, check with the estate attorney to make sure this is consistent with the estate plan.

f. *Partnerships:* Obtain copies of the partnership documents. Have the estate attorney review them to make sure all are in good order. Do the partnership agreements contain the desirable tax elections?

g. *Real estate:* Check the deeds or other title documents. If property is owned jointly, is this desirable and consistent with the estate plan?

3. Locate documents

Often only the individual involved will know the location of important documents, and much time can be saved later by obtaining copies in advance. This would include the will, any trust agreements, deeds to property, insurance policies, marriage and divorce agreements, information regarding investments, etc.

4. Safe deposit box

Check with the estate attorney to determine whether there will be difficulty in obtaining access to the safe deposit box after death. If so, it would be prudent to remove part or all of its contents (particularly the will) to another place.

5. Conduct of affairs before death

If the final illness is apt to be lengthy and business matters must be handled during that period, make arrangements to obtain a *durable* power of attorney so that the proper person can act on behalf of the invalid. Consider whether it would be advisable to place part or all of the assets in a living trust or to revoke existing trusts.

6. Choice of domicile

Determine whether it is possible that any other state will attempt to collect an inheritance tax on the grounds that the decedent was a resident. This frequently is a problem where there is a summer home and a winter home. If so, take whatever steps can be taken to reduce the risk and costs of such a challenge, such as removing property from that state, transferring real estate to other family members, executing affidavits of domicile, transferring property to trusts, etc.

7. Purchase of flower bonds

There are certain issues of government bonds which can be purchased at less than face value during lifetime and then used at face value to pay federal estate taxes. Consider whether the purchase of these bonds would be a wise investment.

8. Lifetime gifts

Taxes can be reduced right up until the moment of death by making advance gifts to persons who would be receiving a portion of the estate in any event. Determine whether the potential estate will be subject to taxes, and if so, consider making gifts. If there is any question of competency to make gifts, consider whether the court will authorize gifts prior to death. Discuss with the estate attorney the criteria and limitations of such tax-advantaged gifts.

Consider advance charitable gifts if appropriate. Such gifts reduce both income taxes and estate taxes if made before death, but reduce only estate taxes after death.

9. Outstanding loans due

If there are any family members who owe money to the invalid, consider whether it would be wise to forgive part or all of those debts before death, if this can be done without making taxable gifts. If not, they will be taxable assets of the estate and must be repaid unless the will forgives them.

10. Debts and other outstanding liabilities

Generally, there is no hurry to pay outstanding debts and liabilities in anticipation of death. There are, however, exceptions to this rule. Medical expenses, for example, are deductible on the invalid's final income tax return; their payment also reduces the estate subject to death taxes. Such expenses should be paid as currently as possible.

11. Funeral arrangements and living wills

If appropriate, discuss funeral arrangements. There may be occasion to have a living will, which is a document conveying a person's wishes with respect to prolonging life under adverse conditions. To be on the safe side, the invalid should discuss decisions about this with his or her doctor to be sure the doctor will honor those wishes. There may also be a desire to make provision for organ transplants, either by provision during lifetime or in the will. A health care power of attorney designating a person to make these important decisions, is preferred by many people.

12. Names and addresses

An initial step in the probate processing is to supply the court with the names and addresses of all the heirs-at-law, who are those persons who would receive the estate in the absence of any will. Those names and addresses should be obtained. Likewise, if there are bequests in the will to old friends or other persons outside the immediate family, their names and current addresses should be obtained.

13. Make cash available where necessary

While probate procedures in Connecticut are simple, straightforward, and seldom delayed, it is always a good idea to make sure there is sufficient cash available for family members who will need it. This can be done through lifetime gifts, which serve the added function of reducing the taxable estate; by establishing joint bank accounts with the intended recipient; or perhaps by making insurance policies or company benefits payable to that person.

14. Increasing the potential estate

Oddly enough, sophisticated income tax planning may make it very advantageous to increase the terminally ill individual's estate. This should never be done without expert legal advice! Usually the increase takes the form of gifts from the healthy spouse to the ailing spouse to take tax advantage of (a) the estate tax unified credit and (b) the fact that in some instances death cancels potential capital gains taxes.

6

Funeral Arrangements

Strictly speaking, before the probate court has approved the will and the named executor, the executor is not responsible for making funeral arrangements, and in fact has no legal authority to do so. It would be rare to have the court proceedings for appointment of the executor completed before the funeral arrangements are finished. Nonetheless, where there is no immediate family, or where the family does not wish to make funeral arrangements, it is common for the executor to assist to one degree or another.

Under Connecticut law, custody and control of the remains of a deceased person are given to the next-of-kin. Usually this means the surviving spouse is entitled to make funeral arrangements, or if there is no surviving spouse, then the children. While the decedent's will may contain instructions or directions pertaining to funeral arrangements, these are not legally binding. Frequently, in fact, the will is not found (or read) before the funeral arrangements are complete.

Although the body is not part of the estate of the deceased, there are certain limited circumstances in which a person may dispose of his or her body or of selected parts. The Uniform Anatomical Gift Act allows adults to leave their bodies for medical, therapeutic, educational, research or other purposes. Similarly, after death, the surviving spouse (or if none, an adult child) may consent to such anatomical gifts.

The cost of funeral arrangements is a legitimate expense of administering the estate and can be paid out of estate assets. A variety of state statutes pertain to such subject matters as registration of death and disposition of the decedent's remains. By and large, these requirements have to do with the work of such organizations as the Department of Health, the Registrar of Vital Statistics and the Police Department. The required reports normally are completed by the decedent's physician and the funeral home. Special arrangements must be made for cremation.

7

Understanding the Will

Wills come in all shapes and sizes and in all degrees of complexity. The most complicated will, oddly enough, is no will at all, because in those circumstances, state law supposes what the decedent would have wished to do with his or her property. Thus a lengthy series of statutes determines the decedent's will.

Approximately 50 percent of the residents of the United States leave wills disposing of their estates. Provisions of those wills, whether straightforward or convoluted, usually can be broken down into these general categories:

1. Disposition of property

It is, after all, the basic thrust of most wills to dispose of a person's property – or, as the lawyers call it, the estate. In many wills, this is accomplished quite simply by leaving the entire estate to a particular person or arranging for it to be divided among a group of persons. For example,

> I leave my entire estate equally to my children.

Where there is reason to treat assets individually, specific bequests will be used.

> I leave my grandfather clock to my brother, John.

Cash bequests also are common.

> I leave $1,000 to each of my children.

Sometimes part or all of the estate is left in trust. One person (the trustee) is designated to manage and invest the property and another (the beneficiary) is to receive the benefit. In most cases there will be an income beneficiary, who receives the trust earnings for a period of time and a remainderman, who receives whatever is left in the trust when it ends. For example:

> I leave one-half of my estate to American Trust Company, as trustee, in trust for my son, Jon. The trustee shall pay all income earned by the trust to Jon for his lifetime. At his death, any remaining trust property shall be distributed to Jon's children, equally.

2. Payment of taxes

Connecticut statutes provide that if no provision has been made in the will regarding payment of estate and inheritance taxes, then those taxes are to be prorated, that is, paid by each person who receives a part of the estate in the proportion that his or her share bears to all shares of the estate. To illustrate, if taxes are $1,000 and you received a $20,000 share of a $100,000 estate, your prorated share of taxes would be 20%, or $200.

Where the estate is to be divided among two or more persons, and the testator does not desire to have taxes apportioned in this manner, it is common to find in the will a tax clause directing how the taxes are to be paid. Usually (but not always), beneficiaries of smaller gifts are not required to contribute to the payment of taxes; their share of taxes is paid from the general estate. Of course, this reduces the net amount passing to the beneficiaries of the general estate. A simplified tax clause might read:

> I direct that all estate and inheritance taxes be paid from my residuary estate passing under Article Fifth of my Will.

3. Appointment of fiduciaries

One of the principal purposes of drawing a will is to name the person who will act as your representative in the settlement of your estate. In Connecticut, such a person is called an executor. If you do not elect to exercise this privilege, the court will designate an appropriate individual, usually a family member, to assume these duties. In such a case, the individual is called an administrator rather than an executor. His or her authority is usually more limited. For this reason, selecting an executor and providing him or her with ample authority to efficiently settle the estate often is a vital step in estate planning.

In addition to designation of an executor, if the terms of the will create a trust, then the testator will designate a trustee to manage that trust. A guardian may also be appointed to assume parental responsibility for minor children.

4. Administrative provisions

The balance of a will, and often the most lengthy and cumbersome portion of the document, will contain a variety of administrative provisions. These clauses are designed to give the executor whatever authority is necessary to settle the estate, and for this reason will depend in part upon the nature of the property. For example, if there is a business to be run, it would be common to include provisions authorizing the retention and management of the business. A further provision directing the employment of family members to manage the business may be included. Additional provisions may be included to deal with various tax situations. Often these provisions are referred to as boilerplate, which is a fair enough description if you keep in mind that boilerplate is what keeps one's ship safe!

8

Selecting Professional Assistance

The inexperienced executor almost always is well advised to seek professional assistance in the settlement of an estate. At the very minimum, an attorney should be consulted to determine whether professional help is or is not needed. The expense of professional assistance is payable from the estate and usually is tax deductible.

To whom should the executor look for guidance? To a large degree this will depend upon the nature of estate assets and the complexities of administration. Professionals frequently employed by executors include the following:

1. Attorney for the estate

In most estates where there is no corporate executor, the attorney selected by the individual executor will be largely responsible for efficient conduct of estate business. While the executor and attorney should reach agreement upon a proper allocation of their duties, it is not uncommon for the latter to assume responsibility for most, if not all, of the technical aspects of probate, tax planning, bookkeeping, and related matters. There is absolutely nothing wrong with allowing the attorney to handle all routine aspects of estate settlement, provided, of course, the executor understands that the ultimate responsibility and accountability remains with him or her.

The executor, no matter how inexperienced, should not allow the attorney to forget who is in charge. While an attorney is not an employee of the executor, in the strict legal sense, nonetheless he or she is accountable to the executor for his or her actions. The executor should insist, at a minimum, that the attorney for the estate inform him or her as to all proposed actions and then report on a regular basis as to the actions actually taken.

2. Bank and trust companies

Where a bank or trust company has been named as a co-executor along with an individual, it is customary for the bank to handle most of the daily routine matters necessary to settle an estate. Generally, this would include such matters as safekeeping of assets, payment of debts and expenses, bookkeeping and maintenance of records and other matters where its professional competence makes the bank an obvious first choice. However, as in the case of utilizing the services of an attorney, the individual co-executor should make plain the role he or she expects to play in estate settlement. The co-executor must also obtain assurances that he or she will be kept current on estate matters and be consulted before decisions are made.

Where a bank has not been named as co-executor, but the need for professional assistance is evident, frequently an individual executor will retain a bank to handle part or all of the estate settlement. This is quite proper. In such a case, the bank will be acting as the executor's agent, or employee, rather than as co-executor. The bank's duties may be confined to such matters as custody of assets and investment advice, or it may have a wider range of responsibilities where the individual executor wishes to remain in the background. This is an excellent arrangement for those executors of large and complicated estates who are concerned that their own lack of experience may lead them to overlook important decisions, especially in the areas of tax planning and preparation.

3. Stock brokers and investment advisors

If the decedent owned securities or if securities are to be purchased during estate administration, usually it will be desirable to establish a relationship with a stock broker, a bank, or an investment advisor. Few individual executors have the experience to act competently in matters of an investment nature, nor do they have the facilities for safekeeping of investments. If substantial charges are involved, the executor should consult with the estate attorney to determine whether those charges affect his or her own entitlement to an executor's commission.

4. Appraisers

Appraisals of estate assets are required for several purposes, foremost among which are (a) the need to establish values for purposes of tax computation and (b) accountability to the court. It is the duty of the executor to arrange for appraisals of estate assets. This does not necessarily mean that professional appraisers must be hired, since many assets can be accurately valued by the executor. An example would be marketable securities, the values for which can be found in daily newspapers. Real estate generally requires professional appraisal, although in the case of property such as the family residence, a brief letter from a reputable real estate broker may be all that is needed. Other assets, such as a family business, often require extensive and detailed professional evaluation. The attorney for the estate will be in a position to make appropriate recommendations with respect to the selection of competent appraisers. To avoid unnecessarily harsh tax results, considerable care must be used in both the selection of appraisers and the actual preparation of the appraisal.

The role of appraisers in reviewing the household furniture and furnishings of the family home is often misunderstood. While it is necessary that such property be inspected and appraised for tax purposes, an important preliminary step is to consult the family and determine which articles were owned by the decedent and which are owned by other family members. After this determination, an appraiser of household goods can be consulted. The market value of used furniture and furnishings is usually nominal; equivalent, perhaps, to the proceeds that might be realized at a tag sale.

In all matters of appraisal, keep firmly in mind that it is the executor who selects the appraiser, not the Internal Revenue Service or any other governmental organization. It is also important that the appraiser be instructed as to the purpose of the appraisal. There is a considerable difference between an appraisal of replacement cost for insurance purposes (often considerably more than the original cost of the item) and an appraisal for estate tax purposes.

5. Accountants

Where the decedent has designated a bank or trust company as co-executor or where an individual executor has engaged an attorney with substantial probate experience, it is most common for the accounting portion of estate work to be handled by the bank or the lawyer. However, if the decedent regularly used the services of a professional accounting firm, often it is more economical to use that firm to handle estate tax and accounting matters. In the few cases where neither the individual executor nor the attorney for the estate has substantial probate experience and the affairs of the decedent appear to require the services of an accounting firm, such a firm should be retained by the executor. Accounting fees can be paid from the estate.

9

The Executor's Duties –
A Broad Outline

In somewhat simplified fashion, the settlement of most estates can be broken down into the following major categories of administration:

1. Application for probate or administration

The formal settlement of an estate gets under way when an application is made to the probate court for approval of the will (if there is one) and for appointment of an executor to take on the responsibility for settling the decedent's affairs and distributing his or her property. (See Appendix A, Form 1.) If there is no will, an application for administration is filed, in which the applicant usually seeks to be appointed as administrator. The court will schedule a hearing on the application. (See Appendix A, Form 2.) If there are no objections from interested persons, the will (if there is one) will be approved and the executor or administrator authorized to begin settlement of the estate. (See Appendix A, Form 3.)

2. Collection and safekeeping of assets

It is the executor's duty to take charge of all assets of the decedent which are a part of his or her estate. The exact steps to be taken will vary according to the nature of the assets.

For example, bank accounts may be transferred into the executor's name, as may be stocks and bonds and similar types of property interests for which there is written evidence of ownership. Real estate, on the other hand, generally passes directly to the beneficiaries of the estate, and an executor has only temporary and limited rights of possession and control. Many assets, such as household furniture and furnishings, have no title papers or other evidences of ownership, and the executor simply exercises control over such property by arranging for its safekeeping and custody.

3. Settlement of creditors' claims and related matters

At the time the executor is appointed, the clerk of the probate court also will publish a notice in a local newspaper, notifying all persons who have claims against the estate to present them to the executor. (See Appendix A, Form 4.) Each claim thereafter presented to the executor must be carefully reviewed and either paid or rejected.

There are two paths an executor may follow with respect to known and unknown claims against the estate. The path of least resistance is simply to allow creditors to present their claims without making any particular effort to notify or not to notify either known, unknown or possibly ascertainable creditors. If this path is followed, Connecticut statutes provide that after 150 days from the appointment of the executor, the assets of the estate may be distributed, and the executor will have no further obligation to creditors who have not yet presented their claims.

Creditors who have not presented their claims are still free to present them, but if all the assets of the estate have been distributed, the claims must now be presented against the beneficiaries of the estate, not the executor. All claims of creditors will continue to be legally valid and must be paid by the beneficiaries (or by the executor, to the extent he or she still has possession of estate assets) so long as the claims are filed within the normal statute of limitations applicable to such claims.

In the alternative, an executor may choose to actually contact known creditors and notify them that they have only a certain amount of time to present their claims or their claims will be barred. This type of active notice to creditors may be useful to avoid continuing uncertainties.

4. Inventory of estate assets

The executor is required to file with the probate court a complete list of all assets of the decedent (an inventory) together with the values of those assets at the date of death. (See Appendix A, Form 5.) Gathering this information may take considerable time. Again, the nature of each asset will determine the formalities of appraisal. Stocks and bonds which are regularly traded are valued at the price traded on the date of death, which usually can be found in the *Wall Street Journal* or other financial newspapers. Other assets, such as household furnishings or real estate, will require written appraisals from experts. Bank account balances at the date of death can be obtained by writing to the respective banks.

When all this information has been gathered, an inventory form must be completed and filed with the probate court. The statutory deadline for filing is two months after the executor is appointed, but in larger estates most courts do not insist that the inventory be filed until the death tax returns are due, nine months after death.

5. Development of income tax plan for estate

For larger estates, it is vital to develop an overall plan to minimize income taxes. There always will be at least two taxpayers available to share the burden of income taxes; the estate (which itself is a separate taxpayer) and the beneficiary of the estate. Where there are several beneficiaries, and particularly where there are trusts involved, opportunities exist for very substantial tax savings. Development of what is generally called the postmortem income tax plan consists, for the most part, of assembling information with respect to expected taxable income of the estate, dates of receipt, expected deductions and dates of payment and expected distributions. This mass of data is then correlated with an appropriate tax year for the estate and the timing of interim and final distributions.

An income tax return for the estate must be filed each year. If the executor elects to use a calendar year for tax purposes, the return is due on each April 15. The executor also will be required to file the decedent's final income tax for the year of death as well as income tax returns which have not yet been filed for any years prior to death.

6. Sales of estate assets

While, in general, an executor has considerable discretion whether to sell or keep estate assets which have not been specifically left to a beneficiary, nonetheless, sale must be considered if (1) it is necessary to raise cash in order to pay taxes, debts, legacies, etc., (2) there are assets which are in danger of rapid decrease in value due to market conditions or otherwise, or (3) there are assets which must be divided among several beneficiaries, but the nature of the assets is such that it would be impractical to divide them, thus suggesting sale and distribution of the resulting cash.

7. Investment of estate assets

Almost all estates will have certain amounts of cash available for temporary investment until needed to pay taxes, debts, expenses, or for distribution. It is the executor's duty to keep these funds prudently invested. However, the executor is not expected to be a speculator. Usually, new estate investments are made in very secure marketable properties, such as United States government bonds, certificates of deposit, money market funds, and the like.

8. Preparation of death tax returns

The executor has two principal death tax returns to prepare, assuming the estate is large enough to require such returns. These are the Connecticut succession tax return and the federal estate death tax return. Both returns are due nine months after the date of death; the Connecticut succession tax must be *paid* at six months after death, however. The federal estate tax is not due until nine months after death. A number of other death tax returns may also be due, depending upon the size and nature of the estate and the location of estate assets.

9. Final administration account

After settlement of the estate is concluded, the executor files with the court a complete statement of his or her activities. This statement, termed the final account (see Appendix G), will show all assets coming into the hands of the executor; the payment of debts, payment of claims and taxes, a list of sales and purchases and a proposed final distribution of remaining estate assets as directed by the decedent's will, or, if there is no will, by Connecticut's laws of intestacy. (See Appendix F.)

The court will schedule a hearing after the final account is filed, so that interested parties may have an opportunity to object to the way the estate was settled. Assuming there are no objections, the probate judge will issue a decree approving the administration account and the ascertainment of the beneficiaries or heirs and will order distribution of the estate's assets.

10. Final distribution

There is a 30-day waiting period after the judge issues the order of distribution during which objections may be filed. After the 30-day waiting period is over, the executor is free to distribute the estate assets. In most cases some paperwork is required to transfer title. The nature of these steps will depend upon the particular assets, and will range from notification of a transfer agent in the case of securities to re-registration of automobiles with the Department of Motor Vehicles. Following final distribution, the executor files an affidavit of closing statement with the court, reporting successful conclusion of estate administration. (See Appendix A, Form 8.)

10

Probating the Will

The process by which a decedent's will is approved by the court and the appointment of an executor is confirmed is known as probating the will. Required information is summarized in a pre-printed form available from the court. (See Appendix A, Form 1.) The completed application for probate and the will generally are delivered to the court promptly after death, so that estate settlement can be started. State law requires delivery of the will within 30 days of death.

The clerk of the court, upon receipt of the will and the application for probate, will schedule a date on which the judge will hold a hearing to determine the validity of the will and to hear any objections to the qualification of the named executor. Anyone who might have an interest in objecting to the probate of the will is entitled to receive notice of this initial hearing. (See Appendix A, Form 2.) If all persons interested in the estate sign written waivers of their right to notice, the will can be probated immediately.

It would be unusual for the beneficiaries of the will to object to its approval, and therefore notice is required to be given only to the heirs-at-law. These are the persons who would receive the estate if the will were not valid; that is, those persons who are the intestate distributees of the estate under the laws of Connecticut. In the most common situation, the persons who would receive an estate in the absence of a valid will are the surviving spouse and the decedent's children. For more complicated family situations, you can refer to Chapter 19, which lists in some detail how intestate estates are distributed under varying circumstances.

In Connecticut, children and other blood relatives of the decedent have no interest in his or her estate once it is determined that there is a valid will, unless they are provided for in the will itself. Only a surviving spouse has absolute rights of inheritance. Those rights are quite limited and are described in Chapter 12. For this reason, it is pointless to provide in the will that a child or other relative shall "receive $1.00." Because children have no right to demand a share of the estate, nothing is accomplished by leaving them a small amount.

In the next chapter we will discuss procedures in the event of any dispute over the will. However, in the vast majority of cases there is no controversy, and the court hearing is a mere formality which is seldom attended by anyone other than the estate attorney and the probate judge.

Once the hearing has been held, the will admitted to probate and the named executor confirmed, the executor can begin settling the estate. An early step is to give written notice to all of the beneficiaries of the will. This is done by the clerk of the court. The executor or his or her attorney is required to supply addresses and mailing envelopes. The clerk also gives notice to all potential creditors of the estate, usually by publication of a Notice to Creditors in the local newspaper. (See Appendix A, Form 4.) This procedure is described in more detail in Chapter 15.

The executor or administrator must also post a bond. This is a financial guarantee that the fiduciary will perform all duties properly, and if not, that any loss to the estate will be made good. A bank which acts as executor need not post a bond and the testator may, in the will, excuse the executor from posting a bond.

11

Disputes over the Will

As we noted in the preceding chapter, an early step in the proceedings for settlement of an estate is to hold a court hearing at which the validity of the will is determined. Briefly, a valid will in this state is one in which:

1. The decedent was an adult, i.e., over age 18.
2. The will was in writing and signed by the decedent.
3. There were at least two witnesses present at the signing of the will; each must have signed the will in the presence of the decedent and each other.
4. The decedent was of sound mind.

Undoubtedly there are many disappointments when the contents of a will are made public to the decedent's family and others, but fights over the will are much rarer than the public is lead to believe by newspaper publicity and works of fiction. From the legal point of view, the predominant reason for lack of will contests is that relatively few people have any right to challenge the contents of the will. Generally, such challenges must take one of the following forms:

1. Contest by an heir-at-law. As described in Chapter 10, there are certain persons who are entitled to share in a decedent's estate if he or she does not leave a valid will, or leaves no will at all. In most cases this will be the decedent's surviving spouse and children. If one of these persons has reason to believe that the will is invalid, he or she has a statutory right to challenge its validity. That challenge must be based upon one of the grounds described earlier. However, unless an obvious mistake has been made in preparing the will (for example, the decedent signed his or her will at home and failed to have it signed by witnesses), success in such a contested proceeding usually will depend upon the ability of the disappointed heir to show that the decedent was improperly influenced by someone or was coerced into signing the will, or was not of sound mind.

A complete discussion of the grounds for such litigation obviously is not within the scope of this book. However, it is worth pointing out that undue influence is very difficult to prove, as it usually involves abuse of a confidential relationship rather than simply one relative being treated more generously than another. Likewise, examples of wills being signed under duress, such as at gunpoint, are quite rare.

The most common ground for will contest is lack of mental capacity resulting from old age or an infirmity like Alzheimer's disease. Even these cases are very difficult to prove. In Connecticut the test for mental capacity is little more than whether the testator knew he or she was signing a will. For example, a person who is so incapable of managing business affairs that it has been necessary to have the court declare incompetency and appoint a conservator, may still be sufficiently capable of knowing what business he or she is about when signing a will.

2. *Will construction suits.* There is a different proceeding involved where the validity of the will is not challenged, but rather one or more of the beneficiaries of the will question its meaning. Many examples of this type of proceeding are found

where the testator has drawn his or her own will and has not understood the legal implications of the chosen language. For example, consider what is meant when an estate is left "equally to my children" and one of the children dies before the testator. Does that child's share (a) pass to the child's estate? (b) pass to the child's own children? or (c) lapse entirely in favor of the remaining children? In this particular instance there is a statutory provision which governs (an anti-lapse statute provides that property left to a deceased child not lapse, but instead passes to his or her children), but few cases of will construction can be solved so readily.

3. Rights of a surviving spouse. As will be discussed at greater length in Chapter 12, the only person who has a statutory right to share in an estate regardless of the will is the surviving spouse of the decedent. For example, if the decedent's will leaves the entire estate to the surviving spouse, the children have no right to contest the will on the grounds that they have been omitted from it. On the other hand, if the will left the entire estate to the children, the surviving spouse could file a right of election with the probate court. The result of filing such an election is to have a one-third share of the estate set aside in a separate trust for the lifetime of the surviving spouse with the net income from that share paid to the spouse. At the spouse's death, the trust will be distributed to the children.

4. Creditors' claims against the estate. Various forms of litigation may be provoked during the course of an estate settlement, arising not so much out of any contest of the provisions of the will, but simply due to various obligations of the decedent entered into and not completed during his or her lifetime. Examples would include contracts which the decedent has not fulfilled and which the executor refuses to honor or a personal injury claim arising from the decedent's negligence. Such claims must be defended by the executor in much the same manner as the decedent would have done had he or she still been living.

Other types of claims and litigation can arise out of the settlement procedure itself. For example, the executor might hire a caretaker for the decedent's property and then become embroiled in a dispute over performance of that contract. Such disagreements can end up in court, again in the same manner as if they had occurred during the lifetime of the decedent.

12

Family Rights and Allowances

In Connecticut, only a surviving spouse has any absolute right to inherit property from another person. Correspondingly, a person is free to leave his or her estate to anyone. The single exception is that a surviving spouse, who is willing to waive all benefits under the will, may require that one-third of the probate estate be set aside in trust for his or her benefit, for life. The surviving spouse then is entitled to receive all of the net income earned by that trust fund. Upon the surviving spouse's death the trust fund reverts to the estate of the deceased spouse, and is disposed of as provided in the original will.

The election by a surviving spouse must be made in writing and filed in the probate court within 150 days after the executor is appointed. In order to take advantage of this special right of election, the surviving spouse must be willing to relinquish all rights under the will. In other words, the surviving spouse must either accept the will entirely or reject it entirely.

Can a husband or wife effectively disinherit a spouse, even to the extent of barring him or her from any benefit under this special statutory election procedure? The answer is a qualified "yes." The statute allowing a surviving spouse to elect a share of the estate in trust applies only to property which is "legally or equitably owned by the [deceased spouse] at the time of his or her death, after the payment of all debts and charges against the estate." It would appear that, during lifetime, a spouse is free to give away all of his or her property, and in that way completely defeat the surviving spouse's right of election. In a leading case on this subject, the Connecticut Supreme Court held that a decedent who placed all of his property in a revocable trust prior to his death (he could have taken it back at any time) successfully defeated his wife's right of election with respect to that property. This is completely contrary to the law of many states, but it continues to be the law in Connecticut.

Quite apart from the right to a lifetime trust interest in one third of the deceased spouse's estate, the surviving spouse and any minor children of the deceased spouse have a statutory right to be supported by the estate for a reasonable period of time after the death of the spouse. (See Appendix A, Form 9.) The amount of this family allowance is in the discretion of the court. It usually will depend upon the standard of living enjoyed by the surviving spouse and the minor children during the deceased spouse's lifetime, as well as the size and character of the estate.

If this allowance is claimed, then the statutory trust share (if elected by the spouse) will not be set aside until expiration of the period of the allowance. There is a presumption in this state that the process of estate settlement will not take more than one year, and for this reason the family allowance generally is limited to one year. It may, however, be extended to subsequent years if settlement of the estate is postponed.

13

Valuing Estate Assets

Each asset of the estate must be valued by the executor. This is true regardless of whether the asset is part of the probate estate (passes under the will) or only part of the taxable estate. The method of valuation and the degree to which an appraisal or expert opinion is required will vary from estate to estate and from asset to asset. The tax consequences of valuation also are significant. Here, the attorney for the estate will play an important role in advising the executor as to the best method to use. An understanding of a few basic principles will be helpful.

For court purposes, valuation is an integral part of the accounting process. As noted in Chapter 14, the executor must file an inventory of all estate assets, that is, the assets which pass through his or her hands as the executor, and then to the beneficiaries as provided by the will or the laws of intestacy where there is no will. In most cases, the value used for court inventory purposes will be the same as the value used for tax purposes, and the discussion which follows is relevant.

Chapter 16 contains a discussion of the various estate and inheritance taxes which may be due the state or the federal government upon the death of a resident or of a nonresident owning property in Connecticut. The tax is calculated on the basis of tax returns filed with the respective tax authorities. These returns require the executor to provide a value for each taxable asset. Viewed solely from this perspective, the executor would be prudent in valuing taxable assets at the lowest value consistent with fairness to both the beneficiaries and the government. The range of values available varies considerably, depending upon the nature of the estate assets. As examples:

1. *Marketable securities.* Most investment grade securities are traded on one of the national or regional stock market exchanges. The value for death tax purposes will be the price at which the stock or bond traded on the date of death. Little is required in this connection, other than obtaining a copy of a financial newspaper for that date. If the security traded at more than one price on the date of death or if the date of death occurred on a day the market was not open for business, the tax returns contain rules for finding an average price.

2. *Closely held securities.* If the decedent owned stock or other interests in a family company or in any company which is not publicly traded, it will be necessary to acquire more information before arriving at a value for the asset. The attorney for the estate will be able to assist. Additional information required may depend upon the extent of the holdings; a few shares of stock worth a modest amount of money obviously do not necessitate an extensive investigation. A good faith effort to arrive at a value based upon the most recent financial statements for the company probably will be sufficient. On the other hand, a substantial interest in a large privately held company may require the executor to retain the service of an independent appraisal firm to prepare a comprehensive and detailed appraisal. In such circumstances the appraisal, particularly if the value is chosen for death tax purposes, will affect income taxes due later.

3. *Real estate.* It will almost always be necessary for the executor to retain a real estate broker to prepare at least a brief

appraisal of such property. If commercial real estate is involved, a more detailed appraisal may be needed in order to take into account the terms of any lease. Again, income tax considerations must be weighed against death tax objectives.

4. *Bank accounts.* Usually a letter from the bank giving the executor the date-of-death balance will be sufficient for appraisal purposes.

5. *Personal property.* Appraising the furniture and furnishings of the family home, personal effects of the decedent, and such items as jewelry, clothing, and the like, can pose significant problems for the executor. If there is a substantial amount of this type of property, a professional appraisal firm should be employed. The necessary qualifications of such a firm will depend upon the quality of the assets. In most instances, local auction houses or even the groups which run tag sales will have sufficient expertise to do the job. But if there are important art objects, valuable collections, or antiques, highly qualified professional appraisers may be needed both for tax purposes and to determine eventual distribution.

Often, this type of property is left in equal shares to children or other groups of family relatives. The appraisals will be useful, not only for tax purposes, but also to enable the beneficiaries to allocate the items among themselves.

This list of properties is not meant to be exhaustive, but only to indicate some of the problems which arise in connection with appraisal and valuation. If there are federal tax problems involved, as well as probate and state tax problems, the process of appraisal becomes even more difficult.

14

Preparing the Inventory
of Estate Assets

Among the most basic responsibilities of the executor is to deliver the estate assets to the beneficiaries after payment of all outstanding debts, expenses and taxes. As we will see in Chapter 25, the only way in which the estate beneficiaries can be certain that the executor has carried out this responsibility is to have available a complete report of his or her activities in settling the estate. Under Connecticut law, this report to the beneficiaries is referred to as an accounting and is filed in the probate court.

An accounting, of course, must proceed from a starting point. This starting point is known as the inventory. The probate court inventory consists of a complete list of all assets which were owned in the decedent's own name and, therefore, have come into the hands of the executor. It also includes such items as life insurance payable to the estate, but not property owned jointly with right of survivorship. The inventory must provide a description of each asset, including its value at the date of the decedent's death. Pre-printed forms suitable for use in preparing an inventory can be obtained from the local probate court. (See Appendix A, Form 5.)

The statutes of this state require that the executor file the inventory in the probate court within two months after appointment. The probate court may remove the executor for failure to comply with this statutory requirement. However, in many courts it is recognized that preparation of the inventory often requires a considerable amount of fact-gathering which cannot reasonably be completed within two months, and it would be inefficient to require an incomplete inventory so soon. Therefore, it is customary in these probate courts to accept the filing of an inventory at the same time the state and federal tax returns are filed or approximately nine months after the date of death. This is most efficient from an accounting and administrative standpoint, since preparation of the tax returns and preparation of the probate court inventory overlap to a considerable degree.

In valuing the assets reported on the inventory, the executor should consider the advisability of employing professional assistance. Certain assets, such as marketable securities, can readily be valued using the *Wall Street Journal* or other sources of financial information. Other assets, such as real estate, ordinarily cannot be valued without employing professional appraisers. The Internal Revenue Service and the Department of Revenue Services usually require professional appraisals of such assets in any event. It should be noted that in Connecticut there is no system of court-appointed appraisers; the decision to hire appraisers and the selection of appraisers are entirely within the discretion of the executor. The cost of professional appraisals is charged to the estate.

15

Debts and Claims

An important part of the executor's job is to review all claims which are filed against the estate, including items ranging from the balances due in routine charge accounts to outstanding bank loans. The executor must determine whether these claims are legitimate obligations of the estate. If so, arrangements must be made for payment. The decision is not whether the debts are just or fair, but whether they are legally enforceable obligations of the estate. An executor who pays a claim which is not legally enforceable may be required to reimburse the estate out of his or her own pocket.

Connecticut probate procedures require the clerk of the probate court to arrange for a notice to be published in a local newspaper advising the general public (and therefore, at least in theory, all possible creditors) of the death of the decedent and of the necessity that they present their claims to the estate. This notice is informational only. The executor has no affirmative duty to contact or notify creditors of the decedent, even those that are known. However, the executor will be at his or her own peril if any distributions are made from the estate within the first 150 days after his or her appointment and there are insufficient assets remaining in the estate to satisfy the claims of creditors. After the 150 day period has passed, the executor will be protected in distributing estate assets and creditors who have not yet paid claims will be forced to sue the beneficiaries of the estate with respect to those assets.

There is a supplementary proceeding available if the executor wishes to be certain that a creditor is barred from pursuing a claim against either the estate or the beneficiaries of the estate. This can be done by giving the creditor direct written notice and specifying in that notice that the creditor will be barred forever, if he or she does not file a claim by a specified date.

To be valid, a claim must be in writing. The executor may either pay the claim or give the creditor notice that the claim has been rejected so that the creditor can determine whether or not to bring suit. If the executor fails to take any action within 90 days from the filing of the claim, the creditor can file a demand notice, and if that also is not acted upon, the claim will be considered automatically rejected, and the creditor will then have 120 days to bring suit.

If the claim of a creditor has not been finally determined by these procedures, then the beneficiaries of the estate will be liable, *pro rata*, to the creditor.

If the executor has any doubt regarding the advisability of paying an outstanding debt or claim, he or she should consult with legal counsel. A simple court procedure is available by which the executor can be authorized to compromise doubtful or disputed claims.

Within 60 days after expiration of the 150 day period, the executor is required to file with the probate court a complete list of all claims that he or she has paid or rejected. (See Appendix A, Form 7.) The court will review this list and approve or disapprove the actions of the executor. Reportable claims, for this purpose, include all debts incurred by the decedent before his death. They do not include administrative expenses incurred by the executor in settling the estate.

The executor should be aware that in the event he or she has a personal claim against the estate (as, for example, where the decedent owed the executor money), such a claim cannot be paid without the prior approval of the probate court. Special procedures must be followed in insolvent estates, where the assets of the estate are not sufficient to pay all debts and administration expenses. If it appears that this may be the case, the executor should consult an attorney before paying any bills, as some are entitled to payment before others.

16

Taxes

While not every estate is required to pay taxes, one of the executor's most important responsibilities is to determine whether taxes are due, what taxes are due, in what amounts, and when they must be paid. Usually professional assistance is necessary to make these decisions. Once made, the next responsibility of the executor is to raise the necessary cash to pay the taxes when due and to invest it safely until that date. Finally, after the tax returns are filed and the taxes paid, it continues to be the executor's responsibility to participate in any audits of the tax returns required by the government, to negotiate appropriate settlements, file any necessary amended tax returns and pay tax deficiencies. A thorough understanding of tax law and procedures is essential, not only for protection of the estate but also for protection of the executor. This aspect of estate settlement is best entrusted to experienced legal counsel.

Almost every executor is required to file at least one tax return on behalf of the decedent, and that is the decedent's final federal income tax return. In most cases, there also will be some form of inheritance tax return. Depending upon the size and complexity of the estate, a variety of other tax returns may be required. In the materials which follow, we will attempt to cover only the most basic tax returns to alert you to their existence and the circumstances in which they must be filed.

1. Connecticut succession tax return

Connecticut imposes a succession tax (a form of inheritance tax) on the estates of persons who die while they are residents and also on non-residents who own real estate located in Connecticut. The rate of tax depends upon the relationship of the beneficiary to the decedent and upon the total amount of property passing to each class of beneficiary. Each class of beneficiary also is entitled to a specific exemption from tax; for example, property passing to children is taxed at rates beginning at 4.29 %, but only after the first $50,000. Property passing to a spouse is tax free. Appendix B contains a chart of the Connecticut succession tax rates and other information useful in determining the amount of tax due.

The executor is required to file a succession tax return within nine months after the date of death. Payment, however, is due at six months. Copies of the return can be obtained from the probate court, and the return is filed with that court, in duplicate. For a complete description of the Connecticut succession tax, see Wilhelm, *Connecticut Estates Practice – Death Taxes (Second Edition)*, which is available from Lawyers Cooperative Publishing Company, Rochester, New York.

2. Connecticut estate tax return

Connecticut also imposes an estate tax in addition to the succession tax. As a general rule, this special tax applies only to very large estates or to estates which have assets subject to the federal estate tax, but not the Connecticut succession tax.

The general purpose of the Connecticut estate tax is to take advantage of a provision in the United States estate tax law which allows an estate to claim a credit against the federal tax for death taxes paid to state governments. However, this credit is available only if taxes are actually paid to the state. The Connecticut estate tax is designed to make sure that the part of the tax, which otherwise would be paid to the federal government, is payable to the state instead. For this reason it is sometimes referred to as a sponge tax, since it soaks up the available federal tax credit.

There is a separate Connecticut estate tax return, which is also due nine months after the date of death. It is a one-page form, available from the probate court, upon which the executor is required to report to the State of Connecticut the same information reported to the federal government on the United States estate tax return, so that the amount of the Connecticut estate tax can be determined.

3. Federal estate tax return

The United States collects a federal estate tax only on estates over $600,000 and even then there will be no tax due on an estate which is left solely to a surviving husband or wife. The result is the same in Connecticut, for while there is no "marital deduction" for the succession tax, all property passing to a surviving spouse is exempt from succession tax. One of the few distinctions between the two taxes, however, is that certain common trusts which fully qualify for the federal marital deduction are sometimes potentially taxable in Connecticut because the children have a valuable interest after the spouse's death.

Since the estate subject to tax is the net estate after all available deductions, the tax can be determined only after computing those deductions. Generally, deductions are available for all of the decedent's outstanding debts at the time of his or her death, the costs of settling the estate (including attorney's and executor's fees), the value of any property left to a surviving spouse (the "marital deduction"), and the value of any property left to charity (the "charitable deduction"). A variety of other deductions (and certain tax credits) are available in varying circumstances.

Some examples of federal taxes, after allowing for the unified credit and the maximum credit for taxes paid to state governments, are as follows for 1994:

Size of Estate	Federal Tax (after maximum state tax credit)	Approximate Tax Rate on Excess
Under $600,000	- 0 -	33.0%
$1,000,000	$ 119,800	33.4%
$2,000,000	$ 488,400	41.8%
$3,000,000	$ 916,000	46.2%
$4,000,000	$1,367,600	44.6%
$5,000,000	$1,806,400	43.8%

If it appears the estate you are settling will require filing of a federal estate tax return, it is highly recommended that you employ the services of an experienced professional. The tax rates are so high that failure to take advantage of the applicable tax laws by claiming all available deductions and credits can greatly diminish the estate. In addition, there are substantial interest rates and penalties in the event the tax is incorrectly determined.

4. Other state and foreign death tax returns

If the decedent whose estate you are settling left property located in other states or foreign countries, there may be taxes due in those jurisdictions. As a general rule, real estate owned by a Connecticut resident, which is located in another state or foreign country, is subject to the death taxes where it is located, but is not subject to Connecticut death taxes (in the case of property located in another state) or United States taxes (there is a U.S. tax credit for taxes paid on property located in another country). In addition to real estate, other types of property may be subject to tax outside of Connecticut, depending upon the laws of the particular state. Special attention should be paid to furniture and furnishings or other tangible personal property permanently located in another state and to types of investments which sometimes are classified as real estate, such as oil and gas interests. Where property of this nature is part of the estate, it usually is necessary to engage the services of an attorney located in the other jurisdiction, both to settle the estate under the laws of that jurisdiction, if necessary, and to handle the necessary tax proceedings.

5. *Federal income tax return*

The executor must file the decedent's final federal income tax return, covering the period from his or her last return up to the date of death. If the decedent dies before April 15 of any given year, and has not filed a tax return for the prior year, then there will be two tax returns due from the executor; the full-year return which was not filed, and the return for the short final year from January 1 to the date of death.

Where the decedent was married at the time of death, a joint return is permitted for the final year. To illustrate, if the decedent died on June 1 and a joint return is advisable, that return will cover the decedent's income for the period January 1 to June 1, and the surviving spouse's income for January 1 to December 31. The *estate's* income tax return will report income earned by the decedent which is received after June 1. Both the executor and the surviving spouse are required to sign the final joint return.

While the executor is administering the estate, the estate is a separate taxpayer for federal income tax purposes. There is a separate body of tax law applicable to estates and the provisions are complex. In simple terms, however, the estate will file a separate tax return covering all of its income and claiming all of its deductions for its tax year. It may elect any tax year of its choice, beginning with the date of death and ending on the last day of any month during the succeeding year. This offers substantial opportunities for tax reduction. For example, if the decedent dies on June 10, and the estate receives a very large distribution of income on June 15, the executor could elect a tax year ending June 30. The first tax year of the estate would then be the period June 10 - June 30, so that no further receipts of income after June 30 would be taxed at the high tax bracket applicable to the June 15 distribution. Thereafter, each tax year of the estate would be for a full year, beginning July 1 and ending June 30, except that in the year of final distribution (and termination of estate administration), the tax year would be July 1 through the date of termination.

The above rule is subject to a major exception. Distributions to estate beneficiaries during any given tax year of the estate are treated as (1) deductions by the estate, and (2) taxable income to the beneficiaries, to the extent the estate had taxable income. To illustrate, if an estate had $10,000 of net income during its first year, and distributed $5,000 of stock to one beneficiary and $15,000 of stock to another beneficiary, the estate's income ($10,000) would be allocated to the beneficiaries in proportion to their distributions; $2,500 to the first beneficiary, and $7,500 to the second.

Where there is a large amount of estate income, meticulous planning is necessary to take advantage of the estate's status as a separate taxpayer. It is not unusual for an executor to reduce a family's tax bill by many thousands of dollars through artful application of what has become known as postmortem income tax planning. Again, good professional help is a necessity.

As a final note, while it is not always understood and is frequently resented by the family, the longer an estate can be continued in administration, ordinarily the more favorable the tax consequences. Because the estate is a separate taxpayer and usually will pay tax on its income at a much lower rate

than the beneficiaries, each year that income can be accumulated in the estate represents a net benefit to the family.
Eventually, that accumulated income will be distributed, tax
free, to the family in proportion to their interests. Where such
long-term tax planning is undertaken, the executor should be
certain to explain his or her intentions to the family.

6. Connecticut income tax

Connecticut's income tax is very similar to the federal
income tax. The Connecticut tax return is mainly designed to
report identical information submitted on the taxpayer's federal return. This is true for estates as well as for individuals.

7. United States and Connecticut gift tax returns

You are required by federal and state law to file a gift tax
return whenever your gifts in any year to any one individual
exceed $10,000. However, the federal law differs from the
Connecticut gift tax law in that no federal gift tax is payable
until total taxes exceed the unified credit, or roughly $600,000
of gifts during the course of one's lifetime in excess of the
annual $10,000 exclusions. In this connection, see the discus-
sion in Section 3 of this chapter. The federal estate tax law and
the federal gift tax law are said to be unified; that is, there is
no tax of any kind due until the combined gifts, both during
lifetime and at death, exceed the unified credit. In effect, the
tax on the first $600,000 of gifts in excess of the annual
$10,000 exclusions is deferred until death, when these gifts
must be reported on the federal estate tax return.

The Connecticut gift tax has no unified credit, so all gifts
of over $10,000 per person, per year, are currently taxable.
However, in one sense this is advantageous, because unlike
the federal tax, the Connecticut gift tax is much lower than the
succession tax.

Let's see how this works out in a typical case of Mr. Jones, who has $840,000 of taxable assets.

Year - Transaction	Federal Gift Tax Result	State Result
1992 - Jones gives $10,000 to Smith	No taxable gift ($10,000 annual exclusion applies)	Same
1993 - Jones gives $30,000 to Smith	Taxable gift of $20,000 (the excess over the $10,000 annual exclusion) No gift tax is due because Jones uses up $20,000 of his unified credit equivalent	Tax due on $20,000
1994 - Jones dies, leaving his entire remaining estate to Smith	Jones leaves taxable estate of $820,000 (his remaining estate of $800,000 plus $20,000 of lifetime taxable gifts) After deducting his unified credit equivalent of $600,000, Jones' estate will pay federal estate tax on $220,000, or about $81,000	Taxable estate of $800,000

17

Costs of Estate Settlement: Executor's Commissions, Attorney's Fees, Court Costs, and Other Expenses

It is not surprising that management and settlement of an estate can be time-consuming and, therefore, an expensive process. If the estate is of sufficient size to be subject to either state or federal death taxes, it will be at least one year, and often several years, before the job is finished. During those years of management, the executor is entitled to be paid for his or her services. In almost all instances the executor also will engage the services of (and eventually pay) one or more of the following: the local court having jurisdiction over estate settlements, attorneys, appraisers, stock brokers and possibly investment advisors, auction houses, a funeral home, and a variety of other services. In all cases, without exception, the executor should be careful in selecting the right person to do the right job and reach agreement (in advance) as to fees or other charges.

While there is a wide variety of costs involved in the settlement of most estates, there are three categories which are considered to be most significant – executor's commissions, attorney's fees, and court costs. Let's examine these in turn.

1. Executor's commissions

The Connecticut Supreme Court tells us that an executor is entitled to be paid on a *quantum meruit* basis for his or her services in settling the estate. That's a nice Latin phrase which can be loosely translated as "You're only entitled to what you've earned." Consequently, the executor's charges should be directly related to the services performed, and should be calculated at a fair and reasonable rate, taking into consideration such factors as the skills of the executor, the results achieved in estate settlement, the time required, and so forth. However, the rule of *quantum meruit* is easier to state than it is to apply. For this reason, banks traditionally have charged for services as executor on the basis of a printed fee schedule based primarily (but not exclusively) upon the size of the estate. This is supported by the reasonable assumption that, at least in most cases, the larger the estate, the more work involved and the greater skill required. A sample fee schedule, based upon a recent brochure of a Connecticut bank, might be as follows:

4% of the first $200,000 of estate value
3% of the next $800,000
2% of the next $5,000,000
1 % over $6,000,000

This fee is a one-time charge, not an annual charge. Historically, it was billed and collected at the conclusion of the estate administration, but in recent years the tendency has been for executors to bill for their services on a quarterly or other regular basis.

In addition, most bank fee schedules include further charges (not always applicable in each case) for collection of income, management and sale of real estate, service of mortgages, supervision of family business, and other unusual but essential services.

Where an individual, rather than a bank, serves as an executor, it is customary for the courts to approve executor's commissions of roughly the same amount as those charged by local banks. Frequently the court, however, will not approve an individual executor's commission of the same magnitude as a bank's if the individual has few of the requisite skills, particularly if someone other than the executor performed many of the administrative duties and was paid out of the estate for such services.

Often there will be two or more executors. The courts again are inclined to apply the rule of *quantum meruit* in these cases. Unless there is evidence to the contrary, the judge is likely to assume that some of the work involved in settling the estate was split up among the executors and, therefore, their individual fees should be reduced proportionately. Other parts of the work must be done jointly, of course, and as a result it would not be unusual for two executors to each receive 75% of the commission ordinarily allowed to a sole executor.

As another example, if a bank and an individual are co-executors, then depending upon the roles assumed by each, it's possible that the bank would collect its usual fee based upon the table above, and the individual executor might claim perhaps one-half of that amount and frequently much less. The testator is assumed to have known that there will be more time and effort needed when two or more executors are appointed, so a larger aggregate fee is consistent with his or her expectations.

However, since executor's commissions are deductible for tax purposes, the actual cost to the family of paying these commissions may be substantially less than appears at first blush. For example, if the estate is in the 40% tax bracket, a $10,000 executor's fee will save $4,000 in taxes and, therefore, reduce the estate by only $6,000.

2. Attorney's fees

The fees of counsel to the estate are determined in much the same manner as the executor's commissions. The Code of

Professional Responsibility, which, when taken together with other state law, governs how an attorney determines his or her fee, requires that a number of factors be included in determining the charges. Among these are:

a. The time and labor required, the novelty and difficulty of the questions involved, and the skill requisite to perform the legal service properly.

b. The likelihood, if apparent to the client, that acceptance of the particular employment will preclude other employment by the lawyer.

c. The fee customarily charged in the locality for similar legal services.

d. The amount involved and the results obtained.

e. The time limitations imposed by the client or by the circumstances.

f. The nature and length of the professional relationship with the client.

g. The experience, reputation, and ability of the lawyer or lawyers performing the services.

Nonetheless, most probate lawyers, like most banks and other professional executors, still tend to think in terms of certain percentages of estate assets as representing a fair fee. Those percentages are similar to those in the bank fee schedule set forth above. Increasingly, however, the larger law firms charge for estate settlement on a hourly basis. Each attorney, accountant, paralegal and administrator in the firm will have a specified billing rate for time spent on estate matters. The total charges for estate settlement then are determined by adding the charges for each individual who assists. This permits a more economical division of labor because each aspect of the work involved in settling an estate can be assigned to a lawyer or paralegal with a billing rate consistent with his or her skills. For example, estate bookkeeping can be done by an accountant hired by the law firm at a lower billing rate than most lawyers would charge for their time. The executor should be certain to determine in advance how the attorney for the estate will determine his or her fees. If possible, the executor should obtain at least a "ballpark" estimate – in writing – as to what those fees might be. In fact, legal ethics require the attorney to provide such a statement on his or her own volition. If the estimated fee seems unreasonable, the executor should not hesitate to interview other lawyers or law firms of comparable skill and determine whether more favorable arrangements can be made. Bear in mind, however, that it is as true in purchasing legal services as it is elsewhere, that the best quality is not always available at the cheapest price.

3. Court costs

Few people are aware that in Connecticut the court costs of probate are fixed by statute and are very modest indeed. While there may be minor charges from time to time for photocopying, supplying documents, etc., the basic probate charges are set forth in the table below.

Taxable Estate	Court Fee
$ 1 – 1,000	$ 10
$ 10,000	$ 100
$ 100,000	$ 370
$ 200,000	$ 670
$ 500,000	$ 1,570
$ 1,000,000	$ 2 ,570
$ 4,715,000 and over	$ 10,000

An estate, for tax purposes only, can be less than $100

When you take into consideration that the probate of an estate may require several years, and during that time the court is always available for consultation and assistance, free of charge, it becomes difficult to understand the public clamor over the costs of going through probate. In fact, estate planners frequently use a rule-of-thumb in estimating *all* of the costs of probate, including executor's fees, attorney's fees, court costs and funeral expenses, at roughly 6% – 8% of the estate. Moreover, all of these costs may be tax deductible.

18

Estimating and Raising
Cash Requirements

Very early in the administration of an estate, the executor should make a careful estimate of the costs of settlement. These are sometimes referred to as the cash requirements, as, for the most part, estate obligations can only be discharged by cash payment. By implication, the process of estimating cash requirements also requires preliminary decisions as to which estate assets are to be sold in order to have the necessary cash on hand.

Estimating and then raising the cash requirements of the estate is not only a matter of good planning. It is also essential for the protection of the executor, because the executor is primarily responsible for the payment of estate obligations, at least to the extent that estate assets come into his or her hands. To illustrate the importance of this step, assume that an estate initially holds stocks and bonds with a value of $500,000. Obligations of the estate, including outstanding debts of the decedent, taxes, etc. total $300,000. If the executor imprudently retains all of the decedent's investments, and their market value falls to $250,000, the executor is likely to have to come up with the $50,000 deficiency out of his or her own pocket.

With the above example in mind, the prudent executor will estimate the estate's cash requirements as soon as possible, and immediately sell sufficient estate assets to provide for not only those needs but also a reasonable reserve for unanticipated liabilities. This step sometimes will be met with resistance by the estate beneficiaries, particularly if they believe the estate's investments are sound and have considerable opportunity for appreciation in value. Nonetheless, with respect to the portion of the estate ear-marked to satisfy estate liabilities, it is not the executor's function to invest aggressively or otherwise play the market. Rather, estate property should be sold to raise the necessary cash requirements, and the cash then used to purchase government bonds or some other investment which is not susceptible to significant changes in value.

How does the executor go about estimating cash requirements? For the most part, this is a matter of gathering as much information as possible, as soon as possible, about the decedent's assets and liabilities. Once this information is in hand, the executor can estimate (1) outstanding liabilities, such as the decedent's charge accounts, bank loans, and outstanding bills; (2) direct costs of estate settlement, including executor's commissions, legal fees, court costs, appraisals, etc. and (3) taxes, including estate and federal.

The process of estimating cash requirements can also be used as an opportunity to provide the beneficiaries of the estate with an estimate of their inheritances. You will find a sample Cash Requirements and Disposition Memorandum in Appendix C, which is intended both to estimate the needs of the estate and to inform the beneficiaries of the approximate distributions they can reasonably expect to receive.

19

Distribution and Division
of Estate Assets

The beneficiaries of an estate usually are impatient to receive their inheritances. To what extent and at what points in time can the executor begin to distribute estate property?

1. The timing of estate distributions

The broad general rule is that the executor can make distributions at any time, in any amount, but that distributions are always at personal risk in the event remaining estate assets are insufficient to satisfy legal claims against the estate.

The executor also must be careful to protect the interests of possible creditors of the estate, the taxing authorities, and those who render services to the estate. Premature distributions can leave the executor in an uncomfortable position, for in some respects he or she is personally liable for these settlement costs. The executors can protect themselves against this liability by insisting that any beneficiary agree to return any early distribution if there are unexpected claims against the estate. Yet this runs the risk of the beneficiary spending or otherwise disposing of the distributed property with the result that the promise to return the estate property is now worthless.

In practice, most executors exercise a certain amount of common sense and good judgment in deciding whether it is possible to make distributions before final settlement of the estate. It is not uncommon, however, for an executor to take a very conservative view and insist upon court settlement of a final accounting (which releases the executor from personal liability) before any distributions are made. Usually, no estate distributions should be expected until the executor has acquired sufficient knowledge of estate assets and liabilities to estimate maximum liability. This subject is covered in Chapter 18. After setting aside a sufficient reserve for unforeseen contingencies, the practical executor can begin considering distributions to beneficiaries, especially if they are known to be responsible.

2. Order of distribution

The first distributions to be made usually are the payment of cash legacies and specific bequests of personal property. There is some additional incentive to make prompt payment of cash legacies, since the executor must pay interest on unpaid legacies after one year from the date of death. Consequently, it is fair to say that in Connecticut most cash legacies are paid twelve months after the decedent's death. Earlier payment is not uncommon, however, where the funds of the estate are obviously ample to meet all obligations.

Interim distributions of the residuary estate in any sizeable amount usually occur somewhat later in estate administration. This is because state and federal taxes are the most substantial obligations of the estate, and ordinarily these are not finally determined until completion of the tax audits. These audits require from one to several years after the date of death to complete. Again, however, where there are no significant questions regarding tax liability, an executor often will begin distributions earlier. This is particularly true if distributions will be helpful in reducing income taxes, a subject covered in more detail in Chapter 16.

Final distribution of estate assets can be expected at the time of settlement of the executor's final account. The nature of the accounting process is described in Chapter 25. The usual practice is to file a final accounting showing either an actual or a proposed distribution of the estate, but in fact not to complete the distribution until the court has approved the accounting and ordered distribution. In some cases, particularly if there is a possibility of dispute, the executor would be prudent to postpone final distribution until thirty days after entry of the court's decree. During this thirty day period any interested party has the right of appeal.

3. Division of estate assets

Most estates consist of a variety of assets, which raises the question of how those assets are to be divided where there is more than one beneficiary of the residuary estate. Except perhaps in unusual circumstances, there is no requirement in this state that each and every asset of the estate be divided among the beneficiaries in exact proportion to their interests in the estate. A practical executor will consult the beneficiaries, secure their agreement as to division of estate assets and proceed accordingly.

Where differences of opinion exist among the beneficiaries, the executor must exercise discretion as to a fair and equitable allocation of estate assets. Usually those assets which are capable of being divided without loss in value will be divided in proportion to the interests of each beneficiary. If there are odd pieces of property left over (such as one share of stock), the executor could either (a) sell the stock and divide the cash, or (b) allocate the odd share to one beneficiary, and allocate property of equal value to the other beneficiaries. Where there is no easy method of dividing estate property, the executor must use discretion and often must be somewhat courageous. For example, what should be done if after an amicable division of most of the property of an estate, three children who are equal beneficiaries cannot agree as to who should receive the family piano, the family car and a small interest in a Texas oil well, all of which have the same value? With the children agreeing that none of this property should be sold, the executor might then consider distributing all three assets to the children as equal owners. In any event, it certainly would be prudent to show the proposed distribution in the final accounting, but not actually make the distribution until the court adjudicates the dispute among the children.

4. Receipts

There is no general legal requirement in this state that an executor obtain a formal receipt to prove distribution, nor must any such evidence be filed in court. Often, however, a prudent executor will ask for a receipt where some question of distribution may arise later. In the case of cash legacies, these usually are paid by check, and the cancelled check will be sufficient evidence of distribution.

5. Deeds

In Chapter 22 we will be reminded that under Connecticut law, title to real estate passes directly to the beneficiary of the estate. Because of this automatic passing of title, it is not necessary for an executor to prepare a formal deed conveying title to real estate from the estate or the decedent to the beneficiary. In a sense, however, this leaves a vacuum in the land records; there is no readily apparent method by which a title searcher can determine the next owner of the property after the decedent, because there is no deed or record conveying that title.

In most probate districts, this problem is partially alleviated by the practice of showing real estate owned by the decedent as an asset of the estate when the executor files the inventory with the probate court. The subsequent accounting for the estate will show either sale or distribution of the real estate from the decedent to the beneficiary, provided of course that the title searcher is aware of the death of the decedent and takes the sensible step of reviewing the probate court records after he or she finds no further conveyance of the property on the land records.

Further protection of the chain of title to the property is provided by two Connecticut statutes. The first provides that an executor must record upon the land records a certificate of notice of the death of the decedent, which includes the name and address of the executor. This will serve to alert title searchers to the death of an owner of real estate. (See Appendix A, Form 12.)

The second statute requires that the executor, after the final accounting, obtain from the probate court a certificate containing a description of the property, and naming the new owner. This Certificate of Devise, Descent or Distribution is then filed on the land records of the town or city, and for these limited purposes is commonly regarded as the functional equivalent of a deed. As a broad general rule, the new owner of the property will not be able to sell the property until this certificate is filed, for, among other things, the certificate is evidence that all inheritance taxes on the property have been paid. A somewhat similar probate certificate is filed on the land records as evidence that inheritance taxes have been paid on real estate which was jointly owned with right of survivorship, even though such property does not pass through probate.

6. Distribution where there is no will

In the case of persons who die without a will, their assets are said to pass by the laws of intestacy. These are state statutes which determine rights of inheritance. In Connecticut the laws of intestacy provide that the property of a person who has no will *(i.e.,* is intestate) will be distributed as follows:

a. The surviving spouse will receive the entire estate if there is no surviving issue or parent of the deceased.

b. If there is no surviving issue of the deceased but there is a surviving spouse and surviving parents, then the first $50,000 plus three-quarters of the balance of the estate is paid to the surviving spouse and one-quarter of the balance is paid to the surviving parents.

c. If there are surviving issue of the deceased, all of whom are also issue of the surviving spouse, the surviving spouse receives the first $50,000 and one-half of the balance and the issue of the deceased spouse receive the remaining one-half of the balance.

d. If there are surviving issue of the deceased, one or more of whom are not issue of the surviving spouse, then the surviving spouse and the issue of the decedent share equally in the estate.

e. In cases where there is no surviving spouse, parent or issue, the laws of intestacy become more complicated, and are summarized in the chart found in Appendix F.

20

Record Keeping

The executor has many responsibilities which require complete and accurate record keeping. Among the most important are preparation of the various income and estate tax returns and accountings to the beneficiaries. At all times the executor should be able to demonstrate to the court and all persons interested in the estate exactly what he or she has done with each and every estate asset.

At the outset, the executor should determine the most appropriate means of keeping the estate's books. In simple estates, this may involve no more than opening an estate bank account and carefully recording each check, deposit and withdrawal. Bear in mind that such matters as tax returns and estate accountings may not be prepared for months or perhaps years. For this reason, include a full description of all transactions. Avoid abbreviations and short cuts. What seems perfectly obvious to you at the time of making an entry or withdrawal may be only a murky memory months later. Be especially careful if an attorney or an accountant is going to be reviewing your books and extracting information. Confusing and illegible entries will only make the professional's job more time consuming and increase charges.

The nature of the estate and its need to satisfy various reporting requirements will determine the extent of the records which must be kept. Among those you should consider are the following:

1. Estate checking account

Except in the smallest estates, it is important to open an estate checking account immediately after your appointment as executor. This will serve as a convenient place to deposit estate cash assets, consolidate those assets in one place and earn a reasonable rate of return if the account qualifies for interest payments. By the same token, the estate checking account will give the executor a means by which estate debts and expenses can be paid and final distributions made to beneficiaries. Cancelled checks will provide necessary receipts. Again, do not neglect to include full information on each check stub. Examples of checking account entries might be:

Check No.	Date	Payee	Description	Amount
101	1/5/92	Amex	Payment of American Express credit card charges from 9/1/92 through 10/1/92	$ 150.72
102	7/8/92	John Jones	Payment on account of executor's fees	$5,000.00
103	4/15/93	IRS	1992 income tax liability of estate	$1,010.58

2. Estate savings account

Where there are modest amounts of cash available for investment until needed to pay estate expenses or for distribution to beneficiaries, a separate estate savings account may be useful. However, if the interest rate on savings accounts is not substantially different from that paid on checking accounts, a separate savings account probably is not necessary. Where large amounts of cash are involved, and the needs of the estate are well off in the future, a better rate of return usually can be obtained through bank certificates of deposit, treasury bills, money market funds or similar investments.

3. Brokerage accounts

An estate which holds a considerable number of securities will need to have some mechanism for purchases and sales. Most brokerage houses provide these services at modest cost or free of charge in return for the commissions earned on transactions. These firms also will provide a complete record of all transactions in the form of monthly brokerage statements. These can be very useful to the executor in satisfying his or her obligation to keep careful records.

4. Bank custodian accounts

Many banks act as custodian for securities and provide services similar to those of brokerage firms. This will include collection of dividends, temporary investment of cash, collection of due obligations (such as maturing bonds), exchange of securities, etc. Be careful to check the bank's schedule of charges for such services. In comparing the services provided by a bank through a custodian account and similar services provided by a brokerage firm, however, the executor should consider what insurance (if any) is available through the brokerage firm to protect against losses to the estate. Unless there is adequate insurance, many executors feel that banks offer greater security because of the state and federal laws regulating bank activity.

Estate accounts held at a bank are not subject to the claims of bankruptcy creditors should the bank go under, as they are held in a fiduciary capacity rather than as bank assets.

5. General ledgers

There are likely to be a number of estate assets which are not susceptible to easy handling through banks, brokerage firms, or other business institutions. Yet because the executor generally is accountable to the beneficiaries and the court for every asset owned by the decedent, it is necessary to maintain records of all assets. This includes household furniture and furnishings, personal effects, automobiles, boats, real estate, partnership interests, business assets, etc. The executor should maintain a list of all assets over which he or she assumes control, including a complete description of each. As assets are sold or distributed to the beneficiaries, a notation should be made of each action taken.

6. Professional assistance

If you, as an individual executor, are using the resources of an attorney, a bank or other professional, it probably will be advantageous to ask that professional to keep the estate checkbook and all other estate records, remembering that only you, the executor, can authorize and sign checks. One of the most time consuming and, therefore, expensive aspects of estate settlement is attempting to decipher and reconstruct records which, even if in good order, do not contain all the information needed to prepare tax returns and accountings. If the lawyer or bank responsible for preparing these documents also has been responsible for maintaining estate records, the job will be much easier.

21

Investing Estate Assets

Many years ago the duty of an executor was thought to be solely one of preservation. Not only did the executor have no duty to invest estate assets, if he or she did invest assets and suffered a loss, in all likelihood the executor would be required to make the estate whole. To some degree this principal undoubtedly related to the good to be served by encouraging very prompt settlement of estates. Certainly, if the estate were to be settled and distributed quickly, the need for investment would be minimized.

In recent years, however, the time needed to settle an estate has steadily increased. This is partially attributable to the complexities of modern society. For example, processing medical insurance claims alone can require more time than used to be needed to settle an entire estate. But the greatest single factor in delay is the time needed to obtain federal and state tax clearances. Even in relatively modest estates, it is extremely difficult to complete the necessary tax audits within 15 months after the date of death. More complicated estates often require several years before they can be settled, particularly if one wants to take advantage of as many tax planning opportunities as are available. And, as we have seen elsewhere in this book, the executor acts at his or her own peril when distributing estate assets prior to settlement with the tax authorities. Perhaps more to the point, the probate court will not accept the final accounting of the executor until there has been a settlement with Connecticut's Department of Revenue Services. With these inevitable delays in mind, the need to make estate assets productive during the settlement period is apparent. On the other hand, the executor is not free to invest aggressively, hoping to generate substantial gains for estate beneficiaries at the risk of equally substantial losses. A conservative approach would be to invest estate cash in rock-solid investments, such as government bonds, which guarantee the estate beneficiaries a reasonable rate of return on this investment without risking their inheritance. If a more aggressive investment program is desired, it would be prudent to obtain the consent of all beneficiaries, in writing, before embarking on such a course of action. One suitable situation would be where the executor, after settlement of the estate, will continue to hold estate assets as a trustee for the beneficiaries. In such a case, the continuity of the relationship suggests it is wise to develop a permanent investment program from the outset, after assuring that sufficient cash is available to meet all estate obligations.

The terms of the decedent's will also have a substantial effect on the investment policies of the executor. There is no reason why the decedent cannot direct that a more aggressive investment program be followed during estate administration, particularly if he or she contemplates that the administration period will be prolonged. If it is desired to encourage the executor to undertake an aggressive investment program, the will might exonerate the executor from liability for imprudent investments. While such an exoneration clause is not foolproof, particularly if the executor is grossly negligent or willful in the making of bad investments, at least it provides the court with some indication of the testator's intent.

Finally, it should be noted that by state law an executor is authorized to retain in the estate any securities owned by the decedent at the time of death. Often the terms of the will extend this authorization to retain any investments made by the decedent.

Such provisions should not be regarded, however, as an absolute license to ignore investment considerations. There is little doubt that a court would require an executor to make good any losses occasioned by continuing a foolhardy investment program begun by the decedent, particularly if circumstances change substantially after the date of death. For this reason, it is the general practice of many executors, particularly banks, to review the decedent's investment portfolio immediately after death, and sell the so-called "cats and dogs" on decedent's investment list. Usually this is done in conjunction with raising cash for estate needs, but even if there is ample cash, it still would be prudent to take a close look at all investment properties in the estate.

Occasionally, an estate will contain rare and unusual investment assets, such as gold mines, race horses, stamp collections, oyster beds, and so on; the list is almost endless. If, as an executor, you acquire such exotic properties, and the beneficiaries show an interest in continuing the investment, prompt distribution to the beneficiaries of those properties might well be a practical solution to the problems of retention.

22

Selling Estate Assets

For most purposes, the executor of an estate stands in the place of the decedent. He or she becomes the legal owner of all assets owned by the decedent which pass through the estate, except real estate. No special authority is needed, whether in the will or otherwise, in order to sell estate property. Of course, all sales must be made in careful and prudent fashion.

If the executor is uncertain whether the decision to sell estate property is sound, or whether the price is adequate or the terms of payment satisfactory, he or she should consider seeking approval of the probate court. In Connecticut there is a statutory procedure for obtaining advance probate court approval of proposed sales. The purpose of this statute is to protect the administrator or executor by enabling him or her to obtain advance court approval of actions which the court, in any event, must pass on later when approving the executor's final accounting of his or her administration of the estate.

There are a number of limitations on the general rule that the executor stands in the shoes of the decedent. The following are most common:

1. Sale to the executor

There is an obvious conflict of interest when an executor wishes to purchase assets of the estate. Nonetheless, in many cases, assuming a fair price, there should be no objection to such a sale. This is particularly true in the case of an executor who is a relative of the decedent and perhaps a beneficiary under the will. To reduce the risks of self-dealing between an executor and his or her estate, it is provided by statute in Connecticut that an executor may purchase estate property, but only with court approval.

2. Effect of co-executors

Where there are two or more executors, each executor may act on his or her own and bind the estate by his or her actions. There are many practical problems in following such an approach, however. If a co-executor strongly disapproves of the sale, he or she is likely to petition the probate court for removal of the executor who acted unilaterally.

A harmonious relationship between co-executors is extremely important to efficient estate settlement. Perhaps the only utility of the rule permitting actions by a single executor is the ability to act in the absence or unavailability of the other executor, but with his or her approval.

3. Sale of real estate

Somewhat different rules apply in the case of real estate owned by an estate. While legal title to personal property (such as stocks and bonds, household furnishings, automobiles, etc.) passes from the decedent to the executor, legal title to real estate passes directly to the beneficiary in the case of a specific gift under the will, or to the beneficiaries of the residuary estate where the real estate is not specifically devised. The executor normally has authority over real estate only to the extent necessary to raise funds for the payment of debts, taxes and expenses in the event that other assets of the estate are insufficient. For this reason, generally an executor cannot sell real estate unless there is express authority for such a sale in the will. In the absence of such authority, the executor must obtain a probate court order authorizing sale.

4. *Disposition of proceeds of sale*

Cash received from the sale of estate property normally is used to pay current expenses or other obligations of the estate or is held in reserve for future use and eventual disposition of any remaining cash to the beneficiaries of the estate. During this holding period it is incumbent upon the executor to see that the cash is prudently invested. It is generally felt that an executor should avoid long term investment commitments, such as stocks, bonds, or real estate. Rather, the cash reserves of the estate customarily are invested in savings accounts, certificates of deposit, treasury bills, money market funds or similar forms of investment where there is little or no risk to the estate. An exception might be made in the case of estate funds which are eventually to be held in trust for a prolonged period of time. In those circumstances, particularly if the executor is also the trustee, it may be prudent to initiate a long term investment program rather than to wait for the somewhat technical change of title from the estate to the trust.

23

Out-of-State Assets

The location of an asset (such as a bank account, shares of stock in a company, a parcel of real estate or even the family car) is not always as easy to determine for legal or tax purposes as it is in casual conversation. In part this has to do with the fact that many assets can be picked up and moved, while, at the same time, probate law and tax law require a degree of certainty of location in order to function well. For example, if a person living in New York dies while his or her stock certificate is en route from California on an airplane, it would be rather silly for the State of Illinois to try to collect an inheritance tax on the stock because at the moment of death the airplane was flying over Chicago. An interesting legal fiction has developed to handle such situations. Like most legal fictions it bears a Latin name, *mobilia sequuntur personam*, which can be loosely translated as "movable property follows the person." In plain English, the rule is that movable property will be treated for tax and probate purposes as if it were located at the decedent's home. Immovable property, such as real estate, is considered located exactly where it is.

For practical purposes, the executor can assume most property interests owned by the decedent will fall into one of three categories, with the tax and probate consequences indicated below:

1. Real estate

For all purposes, real estate is located where it exists. If real estate owned by the decedent is located in a state other than that in which he or she was domiciled at the time of death, a separate and distinct probate proceeding generally is necessary in the state where the property is located.[1] Similarly, a separate tax proceeding will be needed in that foreign state. The property will not be subject either to probate or to tax in the decedent's home state (his or her domicile).

While, in most cases, it is easy to determine what constitutes real estate and, hence, is subject to the above rules, there are some investments which cause difficulty. For example, if the decedent owned an oil and gas interest in Texas and died in Connecticut, such property may be treated as real estate, even though it amounts to no more than a right to go onto another person's land and drill for oil and gas. On the other hand, while there is some variation in the law, partnership interests and stock interests may not be considered real estate even though the partnership or corporation owns real estate. For this reason, a partnership interest or a stock interest usually will be probated and taxed in the decedent's home state.

2. Tangible personal property

There is no simple or all-inclusive definition of tangible personal property, but commonly the term refers to that type of property, other than real estate, which has a value of its own. To illustrate, a lawn mower is an item of tangible personal property; a bank book is not, since the latter only represents a right to acquire cash being held by a bank.

[1]For this reason it may be advisable to hold title in joint names or to create a living trust to avoid a second probate proceeding. However, that will not avoid taxation.

The bulk of a decedent's tangible personal property will consist of items such as household furniture and furnishings, clothing, jewelry, automobiles, boats, sporting goods and personal effects. Usually the value of such property is nominal in relation to the rest of the estate, and few questions arise as to what constitutes tangible personal property. Occasionally, however, a practical problem will arise out of an ambiguous provision in the decedent's will. For example, if the decedent, Mr. Jones, was a heavy investor in gold coins and works of art, and his will provides that (1) his tangible personal property goes to his children, and (2) his residuary estate goes to Mrs. Jones, to which portion of the estate should such properties be allocated?

For probate as well as tax purposes, tangible personal property generally is treated as located at the home of the decedent, unless it has an obvious and permanent location elsewhere. For example, the decedent's automobile will be treated as located at home, even though it may be in temporary storage in another state. On the other hand, the household contents of a vacation cottage in another state will be treated as having a permanent location in that state.

3. Intangible personal property

This phrase describes those items (usually investments) which are neither real estate nor tangible personal property. Included in the category would be stocks and bonds, partnership interests, bank accounts, certificates of deposit and (as a more general sub-category) rights to property which have not yet been satisfied by delivery of the particular assets. This sub-category might include such items as an income tax refund not yet received, accounts receivable, an outstanding loan, or an inheritance from a trust that has not yet terminated and been delivered to the decedent.

Intangible personal property also is governed by the old rule of *mobilia personam sequntur*. It is subject to probate and taxed at the state of the decedent's residence (domicile).

Questions relating to taxation of property, which in turn usually are dependent upon their categorization as tangible personal property, intangible personal property, or real estate, are best left to the attorney for the estate.

24

Collecting Insurance, Social Security, and Other Benefits

Many estates consist chiefly of insurance proceeds and benefits available through the decedent's employment. Into the latter category fall such assets as pension plans, profit sharing plans, savings plans, group life insurance, and a considerable variety of similar company benefits. Social Security benefits, while seldom payable to the estate as such, also play an important role in providing for the decedent's family.

Assets of this nature have in common the fact that they are not directly held or possessed by the decedent while living, but rather are in the hands of a stakeholder of some type. This may be the insurance company, the employer, the federal government or another organization. The person entitled to the benefits, whether it be the executor or an individual named as beneficiary, may be required to take some affirmative steps to collect them. Usually this consists of completing and filing a claim form, and providing a copy of the death certificate and proof of the claimant's right of collection.

The executor may wish to take an active role in collecting such property, even though the estate is not directly named as a beneficiary, as for example where an elderly beneficiary looks to the executor for general assistance. The basic steps to be taken are as follows:

1. Thoroughly review all of the decedent's personal papers to determine whether there are benefits of this nature which can be claimed. Often entitlement to a benefit is not readily apparent. Insurance policies, for example, have a way of being mislaid. A review of the decedent's checkbook, however, may disclose payment of premiums. Certainly the decedent's employer should be consulted with respect to the possibility of available company benefits. The local district office of the Social Security Administration will be able to provide information as to this entitlement.

2. The executor should then write to each organization which may be holding a benefit due the decedent or a beneficiary named by the decedent and inquire as to the availability of benefits and the requirements for payment. Prompt investigation of insurance policies and similar property interests is essential. Frequently, the insurance company or other stakeholder is not required by law to pay interest on the funds. Any significant delay in collection will deprive the estate or the beneficiaries of the income which they could have earned for themselves during the period of delay.

3. Where benefits prove available, usually there will be forms to complete in order to apply for distribution. Frequently there also will be decisions to make as to the method of payment. The two most common forms are a lump sum distribution or a lifetime annuity.

4. If the estate proves to be the beneficiary, then the funds due should be collected, invested, and eventually distributed to the beneficiaries of the estate. On the other hand, if family members or other individuals are named as beneficiaries, the executor should notify them of their entitlement. Often the executor will assist in collection.

The tax status of such benefits should not be overlooked.

While certain benefits will pass through probate, that is, be collected by the executor and administered as part of the estate, others will be paid directly to beneficiaries named in the insurance policies or company benefit plans. Whether property of this type passes through probate or not has nothing to do with the important question of whether it is subject to state and federal taxation. These property interests frequently are subject to income tax as well as estate tax, and the attorney for the estate should be consulted in each case.

25

Accountings

The laws of this state require an executor to prepare a complete report of estate settlement activities. This report, called an accounting, must be submitted to the probate court for approval. The court will schedule a public hearing and give notice to each beneficiary of the estate, so that all beneficiaries will have an opportunity to attend the hearing and express any views with respect to the executor's handling of estate matters.

The estate accounting may be a very simple document or quite complex, depending entirely upon the nature of estate assets and the way in which they have been handled. The clerk of the probate court has pre-printed forms which can be used for this purpose. (See Appendix A, Form 6.)

The typical estate accounting begins where the inventory of estate assets left off. (See Chapter 14.) Using this list of the properties which initially came into the hands of the executor as a starting place, the executor then must report to the court and to the estate beneficiaries on what has happened to them. Assuming there have been a variety of transactions, separate schedules traditionally are prepared to list some or all of the following groups of transactions:

1. The collection of income earned on estate assets, including dividends, interest and rent

2. Sale of estate properties
3. Purchases of new assets for the estate
4. Payment of debts of the decedent, administration expenses and taxes
5. Distributions to beneficiaries, including legacies as well as final distributions of the residuary estate

These separate schedules are consolidated into a summary schedule, which serves as the face sheet of the accounting. A sample accounting for an estate of modest size illustrating each of these classes of transactions can be found in Appendix G.

Occasionally an executor will file an interim accounting – that is, an accounting prior to conclusion of estate administration. This is useful where the estate is quite complicated and will require several years to settle, because it permits the executor to obtain court and beneficiary approval as he or she goes along, rather than leaving everything until the end.

The estate accounting is intended to be the final step in settlement. Court approval will be binding on all beneficiaries with respect to all matters clearly reflected in the accounting. For this reason it is important for the executor to describe transactions in sufficient detail so that the beneficiaries can understand them. It is equally important that the beneficiaries attend the hearing to voice their objections, if they are dissatisfied with any aspect of the estate settlement.

Once the court enters its decree approving the accounting, there is a thirty day period within which any beneficiary may file an appeal to the next higher court.

Where the executor or executors are the sole beneficiaries of the estate, no full court accounting is required. Instead, a simple affidavit may be filed with the court, showing compliance with all legal requirements for payment of taxes, debts and expenses of estate settlement. (See Appendix A, Form 10.)

26

Guardians for Children

In many estates a part or all of the decedent's property is left to children who are not yet adults. As a legal matter, minor children cannot represent their own interests; most importantly, except in rare cases, it's unlikely that minors, especially very small children, can protect themselves against mishandling of an estate by an executor. In such cases, the probate court is authorized to appoint a responsible person to look after the interests of the minor. Such a person is called a guardian, or, more properly, a guardian *ad litem*. The additional Latin phrase indicates that the guardian represents the interests of the minor child only for the purpose of this particular probate proceeding.

In determining whom to appoint as a guardian for a minor child, the probate judge will consider the needs of the particular situation. Usually the child's parent will be a good choice, unless the parent's interests in the estate conflict with those of the child. Where there is a conflicting interest or where the estate is large and the parent is inexperienced in business matters, the court often will appoint a local attorney to act as guardian *ad litem*.

The guardian is entitled to reasonable compensation for services on behalf of the child. The fees charged are based principally upon the time spent by the guardian in reviewing the handling of the estate and usually are modest.

27

Small Estates – Special Procedures

There is a special small estates statute in Connecticut which allows the family or other authorized persons to avoid a formal administration and instead settle the estate by signing a simple affidavit. (See Appendix A, Form 11.)

In order to be eligible for settlement as a small estate, the value of all estate assets must not exceed $20,000, and all debts of the decedent must have been paid. Only the following kinds of assets can be handled under the statute:

1. Bank deposits
2. Savings and loan association and credit union accounts
3. Stocks and bonds
4. Unpaid wages
5. Death benefits from a fraternal order or shop society
6. Insurance policies where there is no beneficiary named
7. Personal property, including motor vehicles and boats
8. Interest in a mortgage

The surviving husband or wife has the first right to file an affidavit for the settlement of a small estate. If there is no surviving spouse, any of the next of kin (the nearest blood relatives) may file the affidavit. (See Appendix F.)

The affidavit contains a simple statement to the effect that all debts of the decedent have been paid. The court then will issue an authorization to transfer the decedent's property to the surviving spouse, next of kin, or other persons legally entitled to it. If there is any succession tax due the state, the person receiving the property under the small estate statute is responsible for paying it.

The clerks of the probate courts generally are very helpful in estates where this affidavit procedure can be used, and a brief visit to the local court probably will be your first step.

28

Living Trusts –
The Probate Alternative

For those persons who have chosen the living trust as the cornerstone of their Connecticut estate plan, the process of going through probate (and the duties of the executor) may be only of academic interest. If all property has been transferred into the name of the trustee of the living trust prior to death, then there is no probate estate and nothing to be administered. Even though the decedent may have left a will, that document can simply be filed with the probate court and no application needs to be made to have it probated unless it appoints a guardian for minor children or otherwise deals with matters other than property distribution.

How likely is it that a person can completely avoid probate? For the relatively small estate, it is quite likely. Through a combination of will substitutes, including a living trust, insurance beneficiary designations and jointly-owned property with right of survivorship, it is relatively common for a person to completely avoid probate. There is a minor exception to this statement, at least in the sense that these various techniques for avoiding probate do not serve to avoid Connecticut succession taxes. And, because Connecticut law requires that the succession tax return be filed with the probate court rather than directly with the Department of Revenue Services, there still will be some connection with the probate court even in the case of the non-probate estate. In these circumstances, however, the function of the probate court is minimal.

For larger and more complicated estates, there is little chance of completely avoiding probate. Even the person who is most determined to avoid probate is likely to find that one or more of the following circumstances apply:

1. A person's property interests are constantly changing as new property is acquired and old property disposed of. Unless one is extremely conscientious and meticulously careful, the odds are very good that at least some property will not have been registered in the name of the trustee or through some other will substitute. It then becomes necessary to probate the decedent's will and go through all the usual mechanics of the settlement of the estate although this will not be a particularly onerous or expensive process.

2. Certain types of assets simply can't be transferred into a living trust or made the subject of some other form of will substitute. For example, if an executive acquires stock options as part of his or her compensation, most stock options automatically become part of the estate at the time of death. The will then must be probated in order to dispose of the stock options and to allow appointment of an executor to exercise them.

3. Some forms of will substitutes may be ineffective, as, for example, in the case of an insurance policy designating a beneficiary who predeceases the decedent. The insurance proceeds then become payable to the decedent's estate, and again the probate process must be invoked in order to distribute them.

4. If the decedent has claims which his or her estate should pursue against other persons, it will be necessary to have an executor appointed in order to take care of these matters.

Because it is impractical in the larger estates to completely avoid probate, it becomes important that those who use living trusts and other forms of will substitutes spend some time to carefully coordinate the provisions of those documents with the provisions of the will. One very important consideration is to determine the appropriate source for the payment of death taxes, as it is fairly common for the cash to end up in one place and the tax liability in another.

The usual approach to coordinating living trusts with the probate process is through the mechanism of having two documents, one a living trust containing the basic family estate plan and the other a pour-over will. The pour-over will names an executor to take care of issues relating to the estate and directs that any assets which are part of the probate estate shall be added to the living trust after the estate is settled.

These subjects are discussed in considerable detail in Wilhelm, *The Connecticut Living Trust – Cornerstone of Modern Estate Planning*, a companion volume to this text. In this book you will find examples of basic pour-over wills and basic living trusts.

29

Frequently Asked Questions

Executors often are embarrassed to ask the same questions more than once, even though they did not understand the answer they received the first time. Don't be. Attorneys and bankers forget that their language can be foreign to someone who has had no previous experience in settling an estate. The first few weeks are particularly stressful. Even the simplest explanations often defy comprehension. More often, the explanation is not simple and must be explained more than once to be fully understood. Be sure to ask questions when you don't understand, and don't hesitate to ask as often as necessary to enable you to do your job well.

Earlier chapters have dealt in some depth with many of the important questions. In this chapter we will attempt to give brief answers to the questions which occurred most frequently during our interviews with family executors.

1. The surviving spouse asks, "How do I find out if I have enough money to live on?"

If this is an immediate concern and you have a professional executor, ask that a Cash Requirements and Disposition Memorandum be prepared as soon as possible. At the very least, the attorney for the estate should be able to give you a rough estimate of debts, taxes and expenses. With this information, you can calculate your expected share of the estate and prepare a household budget. If you do not feel like undertaking this project yourself, your attorney or banker undoubtedly can suggest a local financial planner who will lend a hand.

2. What do I do with household bills, financial expenses, credit card statements, etc.?

Turn them all over to the professional executor or to your attorney, if he or she has agreed to assume this role. The executor will sort out which bills the estate should pay and return the rest to you. If you will be handling these details yourself as the family executor, discuss with your attorney what type of records he or she would like you to keep. (Review Chapter 20.)

3. Can I be reimbursed for my expenses as executor?

The executor is entitled to be reimbursed for all expenses of settling the estate, including such things as postage and telephone calls. Be sure to keep good records. The executor also is entitled to be paid for his or her time, effort and services. (See Chapter 17.)

4. Whom does the attorney for the estate represent?

The attorney for the estate represents the executors as fiduciaries responsible for protecting the interests of all persons interested in the estate. He or she does not represent the executors as private persons. If there is a conflict of interest between an executor's duty to the estate and his or her own personal interests (as, for example, when the executor wishes to buy estate property), the executor should consider retaining another attorney as a personal representative. Discuss this subject openly and frankly with the attorney for the estate.

5. How do I find out what the fees of the estate attorney or my co-executor are going to be?

The executor is entitled to know what the legal fees will be and what fee the co-executor will charge. Insist on a written statement. Of course, if you and the attorney for the estate agree that the legal fee will be based upon a certain rate per hour, then the best the attorney can do is give you a rough estimate of the number of hours involved.

6. If I become dissatisfied with my attorney or my co-executor, can I fire them?

Of course an executor can fire an attorney. No explanations are necessary, although that would be courteous. The discharged attorney is entitled to be paid for services rendered to date.

Firing a co-executor is another matter. If the decedent selected the executor and did not give you the right to change executors, there is not much you can do about it, other than to request a resignation and offer to pay for services to date. However, if the executor has been derelict in performing his or her duties, you can petition the court for removal. Be sure to check the will and find out who the successor executor will be.

7. Who's in charge – the executor or the attorney?

The executor is always in charge, but unless you are more experienced at estate settlement than the attorney for the estate, you should exercise this command right sparingly. Certainly the attorney has the right to resign if he or she feels your requests are unreasonable, unethical or contrary to the best interests of the estate.

8. What should I expect (and not expect) from my attorney?

Your attorney is a professional, but is also human. The attorney may go out of his or her way to do things for you that are not, strictly speaking, legal in nature. Elderly or unsophisticated clients often need a great deal of what attorneys call hand holding. Naturally the attorney expects to be paid for his or her services, and you should keep that in mind before asking your attorney to do things that you could do yourself or that really should be the responsibility of your family or other professionals.

9. How do I go about finding reliable financial advisors, accountants, insurance brokers and so on?

If you are the executor or if you have lost someone in the family on whom you relied for business decisions, you should consider the need for professional advisors and the cost. Your attorney can help you decide what type of advisors you need, and will often make recommendations or at least suggest possible inquiries. If there is a bank serving as executor, the trust officer in charge of your account can help.

10. What do I do about income taxes?

Preparation of annual income tax returns and quarterly estimated payment vouchers is a perplexing assignment if you have never done it. Probably the best advice is to retain an accountant or lawyer to do this for you, at least the first time, so you can become familiar with the proper approach.

11. How do I learn to understand bank statements, financial reports, etc.?

Sooner or later, you must make a basic decision. Either you rely on professional advice with respect to investments, or you learn to do it yourself. In either case, however, you should at least learn how to understand the regular statements you'll get from various financial institutions. Don't hesitate to ask for an appointment with the bank officer, lawyer, broker or other advisor, and ask that person to spend whatever time is necessary to educate you.

12. Is it necessary that I understand the will?

Probably the most important thing you should do as executor or as beneficiary of a will is understand the document. While it would take a legal education to fully understand all of the legal terminology, you should at least understand what the assets of the estate are and what happens to each of them under the terms of the will. Ask the attorney to explain in simple language – as many times as necessary.

13. How long should it take to settle an estate?

Many small estates can be fully administered and distributed within a few weeks. Larger, complicated estates can require years of effort. There is no reliable rule of thumb, although it is usually true that an estate can be settled within fifteen months if a federal tax return is not required and no unresolved disputes exist. If you think matters are taking too long, talk frankly to the attorney for the estate. If you still aren't satisfied, go see the probate judge.

14. Must I go through probate if I have a living trust?

If you are very meticulous about transferring all of your property to your living trust before you die, and there are no claims in your favor which must be handled by an executor, then you will not need to go through probate. However, none of us can be entirely certain that we will succeed in transferring all of our property to our living trusts (or indeed that all of our property *can* be transferred to a living trust), nor can we be certain about claims that may exist by us against others or by others against us. For that reason, everyone should have at least a basic simple will in addition to a living trust or other form of will substitute. Parents with minor children are especially encouraged to make a will, for that is the only way they can designate a guardian for their children.

30

Some Non-Lawyerly Hints for the Widow or Widower

You are inexperienced with either the business world or with managing the demands of a home and children. You are also grieving, lonely, frightened and are possibly feeling guilty that you are worried about mundane matters when your husband, wife or parent has just died. How can you possibly recover and function well? Obviously, each situation is different, but some general observations and suggestions may make things easier for you.

1. You are in shock. Some of you are only too aware of the numbness; others will only recognize the symptoms a year later when the pressures ease up. Don't let anyone rush you into making decisions too quickly. There are only a few decisions which need to be made within the first month, such as (a) whether to accept or challenge the provisions of the will; or (b) whom to select as attorney for the estate. Other decisions, like changes in your life-style or selling your house, will be better ones if you postpone them for as long as practicable.

2. Your well-meaning friends all will have advice for you. Some of it will seem good, some conflicting, and some ill-advised. All will be confusing. You may feel more comfortable if you enlist one friend to help you make decisions, but they must be informed decisions. This is the time to pause and think things through.

3. Seek some professional advice at the outset, even if it is just one visit to a first-rate estate and trust attorney to get a frame-work for what has to be done, when it must be done, and what some of your options are.

4. Don't be afraid to ask questions. Sometimes you will need to ask the same question more than once because, due to shock and inexperience, your initial understanding of the answer will be less than perfect. Be wary of the pitfall of neglecting to ask questions because you might appear stupid to your attorney. You won't. The things which have to be done are often esoteric, and your professional advisors themselves continually update their knowledge as laws change. Even if you are experienced in the business world, you will probably have some misconceptions or misinformation about probate. The intelligent executor is aware of this and asks. The inexperienced person, often the widow, is sometimes reluctant to ask and expose her ignorance of business matters, or may not be assertive enough to ask any questions at all. Ask questions; the good attorney will be happy to respond. If not, you may need to find a new attorney. It is not sufficient that a probate attorney be technically proficient; he or she must also be able to communicate with you.

5. Many women in today's society have been shorn of their sense of entitlement. They are insecure, feel they have no right to inherit, to speak up, to challenge advice or even ask questions. If this is true for you, a course in assertiveness training at the local "Y" may be helpful, not just to help you settle the estate, but to help you for the rest of your life.

6. Inexperienced widows frequently say they don't even know the right questions to ask. How can you begin to educate yourself? Talk with your friends. Look for course offerings at your local "Y," community center, community college or adult education center.

7. Grieving may get in the way of some of the difficult financial decisions you have to make. A good financial advisor or attorney will be compassionate and supportive, but you would do better to seek the emotional support you need from other sources. It can be an expensive proposition at today's hourly rates, especially so because an attorney has had no psychological training and is not the professional who can give you the kind of help you need in learning to cope with the most difficult adjustment you may ever have to make. Talk to your clergyman or your doctor. Either should be able to refer you to a psychiatrist or psychologist or one of the support groups that exist for recently bereaved people in almost every community. A few visits at the beginning may help ease your pain and prevent future problems from arising.

Another good source of comfort is your friends. Most of them really want to do something to help. Take them up on their offers. Your friends are sincere when they offer to help and feel helpless unless you let them. You won't be a burden. If your positions were reversed, wouldn't you feel honored if your friend turned to you?

8. When dealing with any of the professionals who will be helping you, make a list of the questions you want to ask before you telephone or go in for an appointment. This benefits you in two ways. You won't forget to ask something important and your bills will be lower.

9. Take care of yourself physically. Force yourself to eat properly. Invite a friend over to share a meal if that is necessary to get you to cook one. That will also keep you from becoming too withdrawn.

Try to get a normal amount of sleep. If you are beginning to sleep too much, force yourself out of bed, away from the television set. Conversely, if you have become an insomniac, force yourself to go to bed at your normal hour, and don't forget the relaxants of a warm bath or warm glass of milk. You will reduce the length of time for the inevitable sleep disturbances if you do so.

Most important, get regular exercise. Make it as vigorous as your health will permit. Find time for physical activity even if you have to cut out something else. Anger, tension and frustration need to be worked off. Only you can do it.

10. Finally, don't give up. Work at it. Struggle with the myriad decisions. Keeping busy will help the grief go away quicker. At the same time it helps you learn to become independent. You will make it!

Appendix A

SAMPLE PROBATE COURT FORMS
USED IN SETTLING AN ESTATE

Titles appear here as referred to in text. Official
titles of forms are in italics if there is a difference.

Form 1 Application for Probate   110
(Application Administration or Probate of Will)

Form 2 Notice of Hearing   112

Form 3 Certificate of Executor's Appointment   113
(Fiduciary's Probate Certificate)

Form 4 Notice to Creditors   114
(Newspaper Notice to Creditors and Return)

Form 5 Inventory   116

Form 6 Accounting   118
(Decedent's Estate Administration Account)

Form 7 Return and List of Creditors' Claims   120
(Return of Claims and List of Notified Creditors)

Form 8 Affidavit of Closing of Estate   122

Form 9 Application and Decree for Support Allowance   124
(Application and Decree for....)

Form 10 Affidavit in Lieu of Accounting of Executor
Who is Sole Beneficiary   126
(Statement in Lieu of Account)

Form 11 Affidavit in Lieu of Administration for
Small Estates   128
(Affidavit in Lieu of Administration)

Form 12 Certificate of Devise, Descent or Distribution   130

Form 13 General Waiver   132

Form 14 Application to Sell or Mortgage Real Property   134

Form 15 Certificate of Notice for Land Records   136

FORM 1

STATE OF CONNECTICUT

COURT OF PROBATE

RECORDED:

APPLICATION
ADMINISTRATION OR
PROBATE OF WILL
PC-200 REV. 9/92
(PRC-16)

[Type or Print. File in duplicate.]
[Use Second Sheet, PC-180, for additional data.]

TO: COURT OF PROBATE, DISTRICT OF Fairfield **DISTRICT NO.** 051 **DATE OF APPLICATION** 9-5-89

ESTATE OF *[Include all names and initials under which any asset was held.]*
John Andrew Smith

SOCIAL SECURITY # 020-28-6102

DATE OF DEATH 9-1-89

DECEDENT'S RESIDENCE AT TIME OF DEATH
[Include full address.]
16 Silver Road
Fairfield, CT 06430

JURISDICTION BASED ON:
☒ Domicile in District
(If domicile is different than residence, please explain.)
Use Second Sheet, PC-180

☐ Other
(Please explain other jurisdictional basis.)

PETITIONER *[Name, address, and zip code.]* 16 Silver Road,
Jane Elizabeth Smith, 16 Silver Road,
Fairfield CT 06430

SURVIVING SPOUSE *[Name, address, and zip code. If no surviving spouse, so state.]* Jane Elizabeth Smith, 16 Silver Road,
Fairfield, CT 06430

HEIRS, NEXT OF KIN, BENEFICIARIES and TRUSTEES, if any. *[Give names, addresses, zip codes, and relationships.]* If heir, indicate ancestor through whom heir takes. If beneficiary, indicate paragraph of will where interest is stated or may arise. For all minors listed, give date of birth. Indicate any person who is under legal disability or in the military service. C.G.S. §§45a-438,439; 45a-436.

John Andrew Smith, jr. - adult son
16 Silver Road, Fairfield, CT 06430

THE PETITIONER REPRESENTS that:

☒ Decedent left a will *and codicil(s)* herewith presented for probate, dated January 10, 1987

☐ Decedent, after making said will *and codicil(s),* had ☐ a child born or ☐ adopted a minor child, ☐ or married, ☐ or had his or her marriage dissolved by divorce or annulment. C.G.S. §45a-257. *[Explain any checked box on Second Sheet, PC-180.]*

☐ The proposed fiduciary, named below, is not the primary executor named in said will or codicil. *[Explain on Second Sheet, PC-180.]*

☐ Decedent left no will.

One or more of the children listed on Second Sheet are <u>not</u> children also of the surviving spouse.

Decedent owned an interest in real property other than joint survivorship in Connecticut at the time of death.

Decedent, or spouse or children of the decedent ☐ did ☒ did not ever receive aid or care from the State of Connecticut. [If affirmative, check appropriate box(es).] ☐ State of Connecticut ☐ Veterans' Home & Hospital. C.G.S. §45a-394.

The estimated value of (a) personal property is $ **300,000** (b) gross taxable estate is $ **500,000**

All the foregoing data is true and complete to the best of his or her knowledge and belief and that he or she has used all proper diligence to ascertain the names and addresses of all heirs and beneficiaries. Any additional data given on Second Sheet is made a part hereof.

WHEREFORE, THE PETITIONER REQUESTS that said will and codicils, if any, be approved and admitted to probate, that letters testamentary be issued to the below-named proposed fiduciary, or that letters of administration be granted to the below-named proposed fiduciary.

(signed) **Jane Elizabeth Smith**
Petitioner's Signature

SUBSCRIBED AND SWORN TO BEFORE ME this **9th** day of **October** , 19 **89**.

(signed) **Roger V. Lawton**
Judge, Ass't Clerk, Notary Public, Comm. Sup. Ct.

PROPOSED FIDUCIARY

IF APPOINTED, I WILL ACCEPT SAID POSITION OF TRUST.

Signature (signed) **Jane Elizabeth Smith**
[Type or print name]
Address and zip code **16 Silver Road, Fairfield, CT 06430**
Fiduciary ☒ is ☐ is not a resident of the state of Connecticut. Fiduciary ☐ is ☐ is not a resident of the state of Connecticut.
Telephone number

ATTORNEY FOR PROPOSED FIDUCIARY [Name, address, zip code, telephone number, Conn. Bar Juris #]

Roger V. Lawton, c/o Jones + Jones, 10 River Road, Fairfield, CT 06430 **312-4084**

Each of the undersigned represents that he or she has examined the application and related documents and hereby WAIVES NOTICE OF HEARING upon said application and has NO OBJECTION to the granting and approval thereof. [If space insufficient, use General Waiver, PC-181. Please also print or type name.]

(signed) **John Andrew Smith, jr.**

APPLICATION ADMINISTRATION OR PROBATE OF WILL
PC-200

FORM 2

NOTICE
OF HEARING
PC-130 REV. 4/85
(PRC-45)

STATE OF CONNECTICUT
COURT OF PROBATE
[Type or Print]

Court of Probate, District of **Fairfield**

District No. **051**

ESTATE OF/IN RE			DATE OF ORDER
JOHN ANDREW SMITH			9-15-89

PETITIONER

JANE ELIZABETH SMITH

DATE OF HEARING	TIME OF HEARING	PLACE OF HEARING (STREET AND TOWN)
10-16-89	10:00 A.M.	Independence Hall, Fairfield, CT

UPON THE APPLICATION OF THE PETITIONER FOR **probate of the Will of**

John Andrew Smith, dated January 10, 1987

AS PER APPLICATION ON FILE MORE FULLY APPEARS,

IT IS ORDERED THAT:

Said application be heard and determined at the Court of Probate at the date, time and place indicated above.

BY ORDER OF THE COURT	~~Howard A. Brown~~
	Judge, ~~Asst. Clerk~~

NOTE: *This notice is sent to you because your interests in this matter will be affected by the Court's decision. If you wish to be heard or seek further information, you should appear at the time and place set for hearing; otherwise, it will not be necessary for you to appear.*

NOTICE OF HEARING

FIDUCIARY'S
PROBATE CERTIFICATE
PC-450   REV. 10/85
(PRC-33)

FORM 3

STATE OF CONNECTICUT

COURT OF PROBATE

FROM: Court of Probate, District of **Fairfield**   District No. **051**

ESTATE OF/IN THE MATTER OF	DATE OF CERTIFICATE
John Andrew Smith	10-1-89

FIDUCIARY'S NAME AND ADDRESS

Jane Elizabeth Smith
16 Silver Road, Fairfield CT 06430

POSITION OF TRUST	DATE OF APPOINTMENT
Executor	10-1-89

The undersigned hereby certifies that the fiduciary of the above named estate has accepted appointment; executed bond according to law or has been excused by will or by statute; and is legally authorized and qualified to act as such fiduciary on said estate; said appointment being unrevoked and in full force as of the above date of certificate.

Limitation, if any, of above certificate ....

IN TESTIMONY WHEREOF, I have hereunto set my hand and affixed the seal of this court on the above date of certificate.

(Signed) Howard A. Brown
Judge; Asst. Clerk

Court
Seal

NOT VALID WITHOUT COURT OF PROBATE SEAL IMPRESSED

FIDUCIARY'S PROBATE CERTIFICATE
PC-450

FORM 4

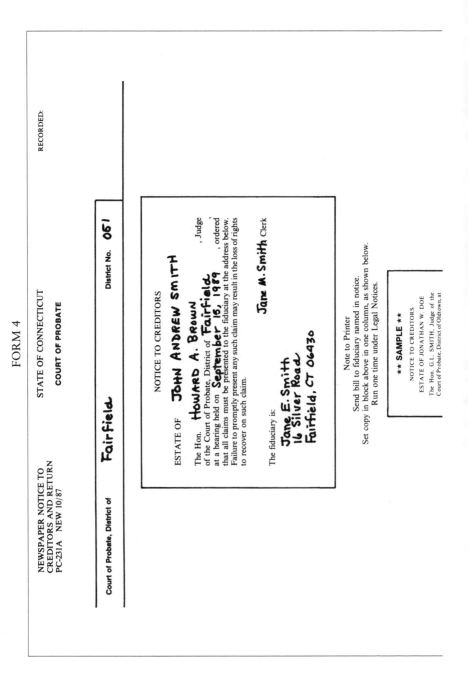

NEWSPAPER NOTICE TO
CREDITORS AND RETURN
PC-231A NEW 10/87

STATE OF CONNECTICUT

COURT OF PROBATE

RECORDED:

Court of Probate, District of **Fairfield**

District No. **061**

NOTICE TO CREDITORS

ESTATE OF **John Andrew Smith**

The Hon. **Howard A. Brown** , Judge
of the Court of Probate, District of **Fairfield**,
at a hearing held on **September 15, 1989** , ordered
that all claims must be presented to the fiduciary at the address below.
Failure to promptly present any such claim may result in the loss of rights
to recover on such claim.

Jane M. Smith Clerk

The fiduciary is:

**Jane E. Smith
16 Silver Road
Fairfield, CT 06430**

Note to Printer
Send bill to fiduciary named in notice.
Set copy in block above in one column, as shown below.
Run one time under Legal Notices.

★★ SAMPLE ★★

NOTICE TO CREDITORS

ESTATE OF JONATHAN W. DOE

The Hon. G.L. SMITH, Judge of the
Court of Probate, District of Oldtown, at

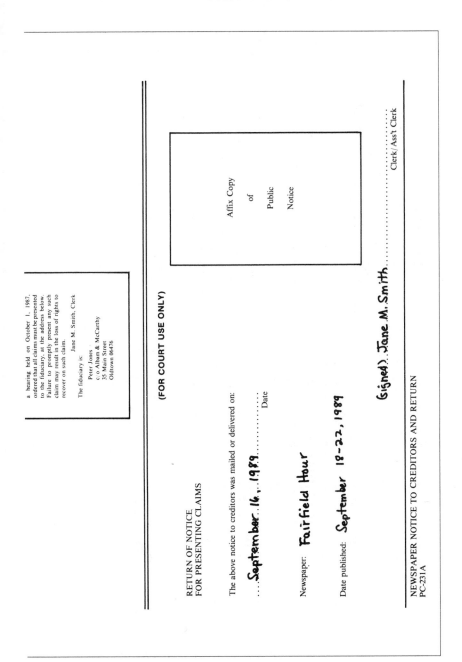

a hearing held on October 1, 1987, ordered that all claims must be presented to the fiduciary, at the address below. Failure to promptly present any such claim may result in the loss of rights to recover on such claim.

Jane M. Smith, Clerk

The fiduciary is:

Peter Jones
c/o Alburn & McCarthy
35 Main Street
Oldtown 06476

(FOR COURT USE ONLY)

Affix Copy

of

Public

Notice

RETURN OF NOTICE
FOR PRESENTING CLAIMS

The above notice to creditors was mailed or delivered on:

... September 16, 1989 ....
                                    Date

Newspaper: Fairfield Hour

Date published: September 18-22, 1989

(Signed) Jane M. Smith ....
                                    Clerk / Ass't Clerk

NEWSPAPER NOTICE TO CREDITORS AND RETURN
PC-231A

FORM 5

INVENTORY
PC-440   REV. 12/85
(PRC-18)

STATE OF CONNECTICUT
COURT OF PROBATE

[Type or Print in black ink.]

RECORDED:

TO: COURT OF PROBATE, DISTRICT OF Fairfield   DISTRICT NO. 651

ESTATE OF   JOHN ANDREW SMITH

Hereinafter referred to as the *Decedent/Ward.*

| | DATE OF APPT. AS FIDUCIARY 12-1-89 |

FIDUCIARY *[Include position of trust]*

Jane E. Smith

| | DATE OF DEATH, if DECEDENT'S ESTATE 9-1-89 |

☒ REGULAR INVENTORY   ☐ SUPPLEMENTAL, SUBSTITUTE, ETC.   PAGE 1 OF 1

INSTRUCTIONS: LIST ASSETS IN THE FOLLOWING CATEGORIES IN THE ORDER GIVEN AND THE MANNER DESCRIBED: (1) REAL PROPERTY: give complete LEGAL DESCRIPTION (copy from deed), show fair market value, balance of unpaid mortgages and net value of interest. (2) STOCKS AND BONDS: show number of shares, description, value per share and total value. (3) ALL OTHER PERSONAL PROPERTY: show account number for all bank accounts; for other personal property use best description available. DECEDENTS' ESTATES: list non-survivorship assets only; use date of death values. ALL OTHER ESTATES: use date of appointment values.

ITEM NO. $

1. Real Property
   Residence at 16 Silver Road, Fairfield, CT   ☒ 200,000
   (description attached)

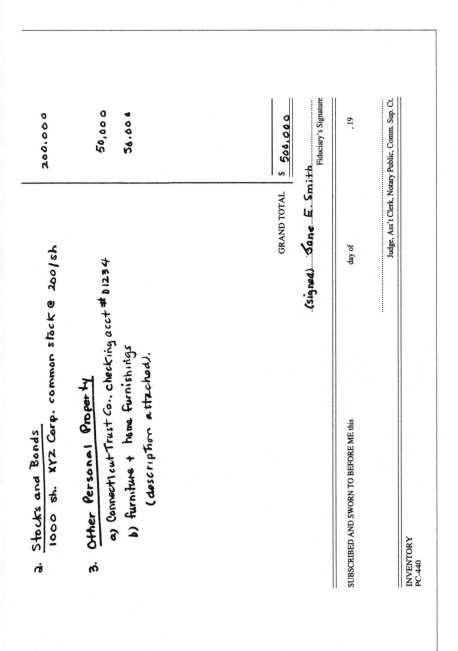

a. Stocks and Bonds

1000 sh. XYZ Corp. common stock @ 200/sh   200.000

3. Other Personal Property

a) Connecticut Trust Co., checking acct # 01234   50,000

b) furniture + home furnishings   56.000

(description attached).

GRAND TOTAL $ 506,000

(signed) Jane E. Smith

....
Fiduciary's Signature

SUBSCRIBED AND SWORN TO BEFORE ME this   day of   , 19

....
Judge, Ass't Clerk, Notary Public, Comm. Sup. Ct.

INVENTORY
PC-440

FORM 6

DECEDENT'S ESTATE
ADMINISTRATION ACCOUNT
(Short Form)
PC-242   REV. 9/91
(PRC-120)

STATE OF CONNECTICUT
COURT OF PROBATE
[Type or Print in black ink]

RECORDED:

To: COURT OF PROBATE, DISTRICT OF Fairfield

DISTRICT NO. 061

IN THE MATTER OF **JOHN ANDREW SMITH, deceased**

Hereinafter referred to as the estate.

FIDUCIARY *[Name, address, zip code and telephone number]*

Jane E. Smith, 16 Silver Road, Fairfield, CT 06430   312-0000

POSITION OF TRUST
Executor

THE FIDUCIARY HEREBY EXHIBITS this account to said court for allowance and makes oath that the same is a true and complete account of all receipts and disbursements made in said capacity.

THE FIDUCIARY REPRESENTS that all claims allowed against said estate have been fully paid; there are no claims now outstanding against the estate, and there are no heirs nor distributees other than those listed in the Application for Administration or Probate of Will or in the schedule of proposed distribution.

THE FIDUCIARY, THEREFORE, MAKES APPLICATION for an ascertainment of heirs and distributees and an order of distribution in accordance with the schedule of proposed distribution attached hereto.

[Use Second Sheet, PC-180 or additional sheets for any supporting schedule]

ASSETS AND INCOME RECEIVED BY FIDUCIARY

To amount of inventory as on file

$ 500,000

To amount of additional property (real/personal) received
[Specify] Cash

15,000

To amount of income received
Dividends
Interest, Account # 02134 .... in ...Connecticut Trust Co....

50,000
5,000

Total $ 570,000

PAYMENTS AND DISTRIBUTIONS BY FIDUCIARY

By claims paid, as per Return on file, PC-237	20,000
By funeral expenses	5,000
By administration expenses	
Legal notices	20
Taxes - succession	23,146
property, real and personal, Town of	4,000
Probate court costs	1,220
Fiduciary's fees *[show disbursements separately]*	-0-
Attorney's fees *[show disbursements separately]*	15,000
[Other]	
Amount on hand for distribution	
Real property	-0-
Personal property	501,614
[Attach schedule of proposed distributees and amounts.]	
Total	$ 570,000

(signed) *Jane E. Smith*

Fiduciary's Signature

SUBSCRIBED AND SWORN TO BEFORE ME this   1st   day of   April   , 1991 .

(signed) *Roger V. Lawton*

~~Judge Asst. Clerk,~~ Notary Public, Comm. Sup. Ct.

DECEDENT'S ESTATE ADMINISTRATION ACCOUNT (Short Form)
PC-242

FORM 7

RETURN OF CLAIMS AND
LIST OF NOTIFIED CREDITORS
PC-237   REV. 4/92

STATE OF CONNECTICUT
COURT OF PROBATE

RECORDED:

[Type or Print in black ink]

TO: COURT OF PROBATE, DISTRICT OF **Fairfield**   DISTRICT NO. **051**

ESTATE OF **JOHN ANDREW SMITH**

FIDUCIARY
JANE E. SMITH

THE FIDUCIARY HEREBY CERTIFIES that the names and addresses of all creditors who were notified by certified or registered mail in accordance with C.G.S. 45a-357(a) are attached hereto and made a part hereof.

THE FIDUCIARY HEREBY CERTIFIES that all claims exhibited to the fiduciary against said estate are set forth below.

CLAIMANT AND ADDRESS OF CLAIMANT	DESCRIPTION OF CLAIM *[If disallowed in whole or in part, indicate total amount claimed and date of written disallowance.]*	AMOUNT ALLOWED
1. American Express	charges through 9-1-89	$ 1,500
2. Connecticut Trust Co.	loan due	8,000
3. " " "	interest on above loan as of 9-1-89	100
4. Electric Co.	electric bill	200
5. Fairfield Police Dept.	parking ticket	50

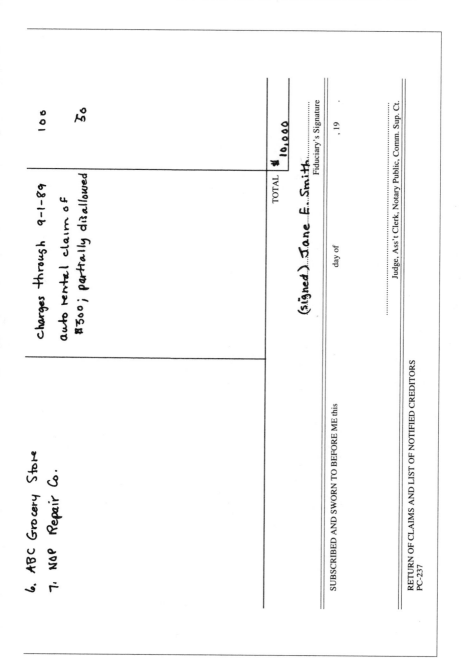

6. ABC Grocery Store — Charges through 9-1-89 — 100

7. NOP Repair Co. — auto rental claim of $500; partially disallowed — 50

TOTAL $ 10,000

(signed) Jane E. Smith
Fiduciary's Signature

SUBSCRIBED AND SWORN TO BEFORE ME this _____ day of _____ , 19____ .

_____
Judge, Ass't Clerk, Notary Public, Comm. Sup. Ct.

RETURN OF CLAIMS AND LIST OF NOTIFIED CREDITORS
PC-237

FORM 8

AFFIDAVIT OF CLOSING
OF ESTATE
PC-213   REV. 6/91
(PRC-38)

STATE OF CONNECTICUT
COURT OF PROBATE
[Type or Print in Black Ink.]

RECORDED:

To: Court of Probate, District of **Fairfield**   District No. **051**

ESTATE OF

JOHN ANDREW SMITH

FIDUCIARY'S NAME

Jane E. Smith

DATE **6-1-91**

POSITION OF TRUST

Executor

The subscriber, fiduciary of said estate, hereby makes return under oath that all monies and property of every description in the fiduciary's hands and control have been paid over and distributed to the persons entitled thereto according to law or the provisions of the will of said decedent and the orders of said court, and that so far as the fiduciary has any knowledge, said estate is now fully administered and settled.

The fiduciary further certifies that the following is a true and complete statement of any transactions since the Final Account on file, including (but not limited to) the disposition of (a) all reserves shown in said account, and (b) any additional income and/or assets received subsequent thereto and not reflected therein:

☒ None.

☐ See Schedule below.

☐ Second Sheet, PC-180 or separate accounting attached hereto.

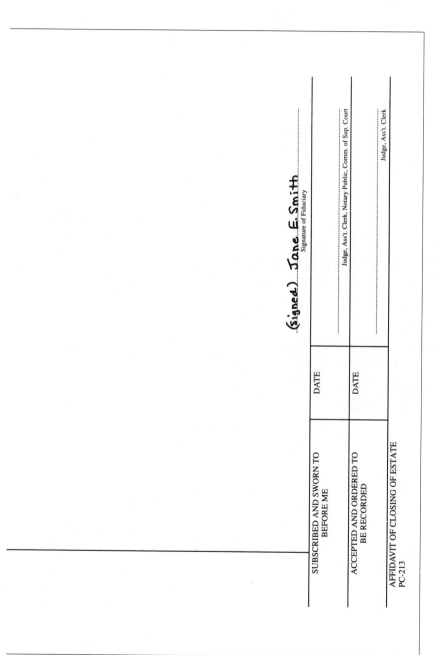

(Signed) Jane E. Smith
Signature of Fiduciary

SUBSCRIBED AND SWORN TO BEFORE ME	DATE	
		Judge, Ass't. Clerk, Notary Public, Comm. of Sup. Court
ACCEPTED AND ORDERED TO BE RECORDED	DATE	
		Judge, Ass't. Clerk

AFFIDAVIT OF CLOSING OF ESTATE
PC-213

FORM 9

APPLICATION
AND DECREE FOR **SUPPORT ALLOWANCE**
PC-202 REV. 9/86
(PRC-57)

STATE OF CONNECTICUT
COURT OF PROBATE

Recorded:

[Type or print]

To: Court of Probate, District of **Fairfield**   District No. **051**

ESTATE OF **JOHN ANDREW SMITH**   LATE OF **Fairfield** , DECEASED

The petitioner is the surviving spouse of said deceased and respectfully makes application to this Court for an allowance
of $ **10,000**   per month, as a lump sum out of said estate for support and for the support of the family
of said deceased during the settlement of said estate.

SIGNED:

DATE: **10-25-89**   (Signed) **Jane E. Smith**
                                                                    Petitioner

The executor/~~administrator~~ has no objection to the allowance of the foregoing application.

SIGNED:

DATE:

16-26-89   (Signed) **Jane E. Smith**
                                                                    Executor/~~Administrator~~

Court of Probate, District of **Fairfield**   District No. **051**

ESTATE OF

JOHN ANDREW SMITH

LATE OF **Fairfield** , DECEASED

PRESENT : Hon. **Howard A. Brown**   Judge

The foregoing application having been presented to this Court the Court finds that notice should be and is hereby dispensed with for cause shown and to grant said allowance is proper.

After hearing held, it is ORDERED AND DECREED that the administrator or the executor of said estate pay said petitioner out of principal the sum of $ **10,000** as follows:

☒ lump sum of $ **10,000**

☐ $ _____ payable _____ per month from date of death for a period of **twelve** months, not to exceed, however, the period of settlement.

☐ $ _____ per month from date of death during the settlement of said estate.

Dated at **Fairfield** , Connecticut this **30th** day of **November** , 19 **89**

(signed) **Howard A. Brown**

Judge

APPLICATION AND DECREE FOR SUPPORT ALLOWANCE

FORM 10

STATEMENT
IN LIEU OF ACCOUNT
PC-243   REV. 12/91
(PRC-59)

STATE OF CONNECTICUT

COURT OF PROBATE

[Type or Print in black ink.]

RECORDED:

TO: COURT OF PROBATE, DISTRICT OF   **Fairfield**   DISTRICT NO. **051**

ESTATE OF   **JOHN ANDREW SMITH**

, in said district deceased.

FIDUCIARY(IES) *[Name(s), address(es), zip code(s) and telephone number(s)]*

Jane E. Smith, 16 Silver Road, Fairfield, CT   312-0000

THE FIDUCIARY(IES) HEREBY REPRESENT(S) UNDER OATH THAT:

☒ He or she is the sole fiduciary of the estate and the sole beneficiary of the residue thereof, that he or she is such beneficiary in his or her own right and not as a trustee, and that he or she is entitled to distribution of the estate on hand, if any.

☐ They are ALL of the fiduciaries of the estate, and each of them is a beneficiary of the residue thereof, that they are such beneficiaries in their own right and not as trustee, and that they have received the distribution of the estate to which they are entitled.

☐ The estate is a testate estate, and the only other beneficiaries thereof, if any, are beneficiaries in their own right and not as trustee, of specific bequests, and such bequests have been distributed and receipts therefor are attached hereto.

All debts, funeral expenses, taxes, and expenses of administration have been paid.

The amount reported on the Return of Claims and List of Notified Creditors, PC-237, on file is $ ....**10,000**............

An itemized list of all funeral expenses, taxes, and expenses of administration is as follows:

Funeral Expenses: $ ......**5,000**......

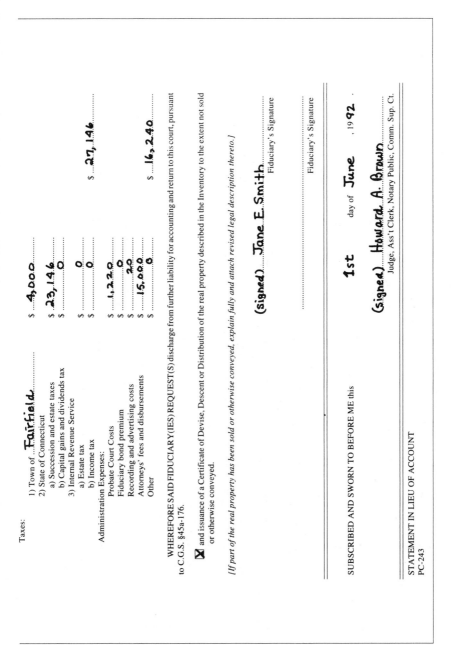

Taxes:

1) Town of ...**Fairfield**................................ $ ..**4,000**....
2) State of Connecticut
   a) Succession and estate taxes .... $ ..**23,146**....
   b) Capital gains and dividends tax .... $ ......**0**....
3) Internal Revenue Service
   a) Estate tax .... $ ......**0**....
   b) Income tax .... $ ..**27,146**....

Administration Expenses:
   Probate Court Costs .... $ ..**1,220**....
   Fiduciary bond premium .... $ ......**20**....
   Recording and advertising costs .... $ ..**15,000**....
   Attorneys' fees and disbursements .... $ ......**0**....
   Other .... $ ..**16,240**....

WHEREFORE SAID FIDUCIARY(IES) REQUEST(S) discharge from further liability for accounting and return to this court, pursuant to C.G.S. §45a-176.

☒ and issuance of a Certificate of Devise, Descent or Distribution of the real property described in the Inventory to the extent not sold or otherwise conveyed.

[If part of the real property has been sold or otherwise conveyed, explain fully and attach revised legal description thereto.]

(signed) ...**Jane E. Smith**.........................
                                    Fiduciary's Signature

....
                                    Fiduciary's Signature

SUBSCRIBED AND SWORN TO BEFORE ME this   **1st**   day of **June**   , 19 **92** .

(signed) ...**Howard A. Brown**...........................
          Judge, Ass't Clerk, Notary Public. Comm. Sup. Ct.

STATEMENT IN LIEU OF ACCOUNT
PC-243

FORM 11

AFFIDAVIT IN LIEU
OF ADMINISTRATION
PC-212   REV. 12/91
(PRC-54)

STATE OF CONNECTICUT
COURT OF PROBATE
[Type or Print in black ink. File in duplicate.]
[Use Second Sheet, PC-180, (PRC-17) for additional data.]

RECORDED:

TO: COURT OF PROBATE, DISTRICT OF **Fairfield**   DISTRICT NO. **051**

IN THE MATTER OF *[Include all names and initials under which any asset was held.]*

ROBERT A. WHITE

Hereinafter referred to as the decedent.

SOCIAL SECURITY #

020-91-3074

DECEDENT'S RESIDENCE AT TIME OF DEATH *[Include full address.]*

22 Seaview Lane
Fairfield, CT 06430

DATE OF DEATH

9-1-89

PETITIONER *[Name, address, zip code and telephone number.]*

Susan B. White, 22 Seaview Lane,
Fairfield, CT 06430   312-1111

RELATIONSHIP TO
DECEDENT, if any

daughter

THE PETITIONER under oath hereby applies to the court of probate for authorization to sell and/or transfer personal property of the decedent without administration or probate of will and states that:

☐ The petitioner is the surviving spouse of said decedent.

☒ There is no surviving spouse, and the petitioner is a next of kin of said decedent.

☐ There is no surviving spouse or next of kin, or such surviving spouse or next of kin has refused such affidavit, and the petitioner is a suitable person with sufficient interest for the following reason ....

No application for settlement of the estate is pending in any court of probate.
The decedent died owning no *real* property, other than survivorship property, if any, in the State of Connecticut.
The market value of the personal property listed below does not exceed $20,000.

The decedent ☐ *did* ☒ *did not* receive aid or care from the State of Connecticut. *[If affirmative, check appropriate box(es).]*

☐ State of Connecticut ☐ Veterans Home & Hospital.

☐ The decedent left a will dated .... which is not being presented for probate.

☒ The decedent left no will.

The decedent died owning the following personal property (*list specific identifying numbers or information*):

DESCRIPTION   FAIR MARKET VALUE

1980 Ford Station Wagon $ 500.00
    Serial No. AB43 70486
Connecticut Trust Company   1,127.55
    Savings Account No. 38417   Total $ 1,627.55

According to the information and belief of the petitioner, all debts of the decedent and claims against the estate are as follows:

NATURE OF CLAIM   CLAIMANT   AMOUNT [If paid, indicate by whom.]

Funeral Expenses   Williams + Son Funeral Home $ 1,750.00
                    (paid by petitioner)

Debts Due for   Dr. Robert Hanet   300.00
Last Sickness   (paid by petitioner)

Other Claims   None

☐ The funeral director has not been paid, and the court is requested to order payment from the assets listed above by a) direct transfer or b) sale of assets.

☐ The creditors to whom debts are due for the last sickness have not been paid, and the court is requested to order payment from the assets listed above by a) direct transfer or b) sale of assets.

☐ The above listed debts or claims have been paid in the manner prescribed by §45a-392 of the Connecticut General Statutes.

☐ Listed assets exceed listed debts and claims, and all heirs-at-law and proposed distributees are listed on form PC-212A attached hereto.

☐ One or more of the children listed on PC-212A are *not* also children of the surviving spouse.

☐ Any attachment hereto is made a part hereof.

WHEREFORE, the undersigned, in lieu of filing an application for administration or probate of will, petitions the court of probate to issue a decree authorizing the holder of such property or the registrant thereof, including the authority issuing the registration, to transfer the same or pay the amount thereof and/or to sell the same and pay the proceeds thereof to the undersigned or as indicated above.

(signed) Susan B. White
                                              Petitioner's Signature

SUBSCRIBED AND SWORN TO BEFORE ME this _____ day of _____ , 19____

_____
Judge, Ass't Clerk, Notary Public, Comm. Sup Ct.

AFFIDAVIT IN LIEU OF ADMINISTRATION
PC-212

FORM 12

CERTIFICATE OF
DEVISE, DESCENT
OR DISTRIBUTION
PC-250   REV. 1/92
(PRC-58)

STATE OF CONNECTICUT

RECORDED:

COURT OF PROBATE

*[File certificate with town clerk
where real property is situated.]*

COURT OF PROBATE, DISTRICT OF   **Fairfield**   DISTRICT NO. **061**

ESTATE OF   **JOHN ANDREW SMITH**

, deceased.

DATE OF DEATH
9-1-89

Pursuant to C.G.S. §45a-450, this certifies that as appears from the records of this court, said deceased died on the date above written, and the following real property of the decedent is devised or distributed or set out or divided or descends to: *[Give name, place of residence, and share of distributee; give street address or lot number of real property, or if none, a brief description of the location. C.G.S. §45a-450.]*

To   **Jane E. Smith**

[description of real estate boundaries]

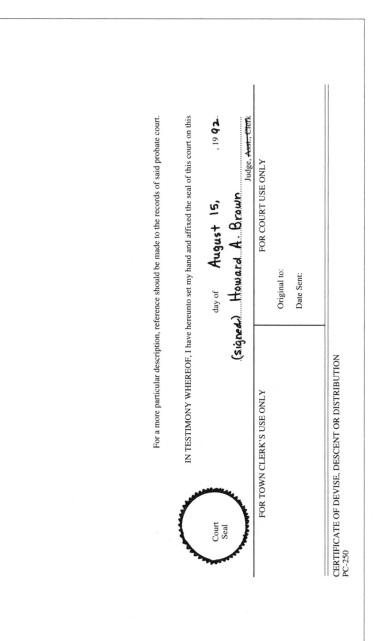

For a more particular description, reference should be made to the records of said probate court.

IN TESTIMONY WHEREOF, I have hereunto set my hand and affixed the seal of this court on this

day of **August 15,** , 19 **92.**

(signed) **Howard A. Brown**
....
Judge, ~~Asst.~~ Clerk

FOR COURT USE ONLY

Original to:

Date Sent:

FOR TOWN CLERK'S USE ONLY

Court
Seal

CERTIFICATE OF DEVISE, DESCENT OR DISTRIBUTION
PC-250

FORM 13

GENERAL WAIVER
PC-181 REV. 8/85
(PRC-19)

STATE OF CONNECTICUT
COURT OF PROBATE
[Type or Print]

RECORDED:

TO: Court of Probate, District of __Fairfield__   District No. 051

ESTATE OF/IN THE MATTER OF

__John Andrew Smith__

DATE OF APPLICATION

__9-1-89__

An application having been presented to the court that:

☐ LETTERS OF ADMINISTRATION be granted on said estate.

☒ AN INSTRUMENT IN WRITING PURPORTING TO BE THE LAST WILL AND TESTAMENT AND CODICILS thereto, if any, of said deceased be proved, approved, allowed, and admitted to probate and letters testamentary be issued.

☐ THE FIDUCIARY be granted AUTHORITY TO SELL real property.

☐ THE FIDUCIARY be granted AUTHORITY TO MORTGAGE real property.

☐ THE FIDUCIARY be granted AUTHORITY TO SETTLE A DOUBTFUL OR DISPUTED CLAIM.

☐ (Other; specify)

WHEREAS, the undersigned are persons interested in said matter and entitled to notice of a hearing upon the application in court;

NOW, THEREFORE, each of the undersigned represents that he has examined the application and related documents and hereby WAIVES NOTICE OF HEARING upon the said application and has NO OBJECTION to the granting and approval thereof.

[To be acknowledged before an officer authorized to administer oaths, i.e. Judge, Ass't. Clerk, Notary Public, Comm. of Sup. Court. [Note: If Notary, show date when commission expires]]

SIGNATURE OF PARTY IN INTEREST

(Signed) John Andrew Smith, Jr.
John Andrew Smith, Jr.
[Type or Print Name of Party in Interest]

The foregoing instrument was acknowledged before me,
this 1st day of September , 19 89.
by

(Signed) Roger V. Lawton
~~Judge, Ass't. Clerk, Notary Public,~~ Comm. of Sup. Court

SIGNATURE OF PARTY IN INTEREST

[Type or Print Name of Party in Interest]

The foregoing instrument was acknowledged before me,
this day of , 19 ,
by

Judge, Ass't. Clerk, Notary Public, Comm. of Sup. Court

SIGNATURE OF PARTY IN INTEREST

[Type or Print Name of Party in Interest]

The foregoing instrument was acknowledged before me,
this day of , 19 ,
by

Judge, Ass't. Clerk, Notary Public, Comm. of Sup. Court

SIGNATURE OF PARTY IN INTEREST

[Type or Print Name of Party in Interest]

The foregoing instrument was acknowledged before me,
this day of , 19 ,
by

Judge, Ass't. Clerk, Notary Public, Comm. of Sup. Court

FOR COURT USE ONLY

☐ All persons entitled to notice have signed waivers.

☐ All persons entitled to notice have NOT signed waivers.

Time and Date of Hearing

GENERAL WAIVER
PC-181

FORM 14

APPLICATION TO
SELL OR MORTGAGE
REAL PROPERTY
PC-400   REV. 10/91
(PRC-51)

STATE OF CONNECTICUT

COURT OF PROBATE

[Type or Print in black ink.]

RECORDED:

TO: COURT OF PROBATE, DISTRICT OF Fairfield   **DISTRICT NO.** 051

ESTATE OF   JOHN ANDREW SMITH

DATE OF APPLICATION

9-1-89

FIDUCIARY *[Name, address, zip code, and telephone number]*

Jane E. Smith

POSITION OF TRUST

Executor

THE FIDUCIARY OF SAID ESTATE REPRESENTS that a certain piece or parcel of land with the buildings and improvements thereon, if any, situated in the Town of ......Fairfield.., State of Connecticut and more particularly described in Schedule "A" attached hereto (*Use Second Sheet, PC-180*),

☒ was owned by the decedent at the time of his or her death.

☐ has been acquired by the fiduciary.

☐ is owned by said ward.

☐ is an asset of said trust estate.

THE FIDUCIARY FURTHER REPRESENTS that it would be for the best interests of the parties in interest to:

☒ sell the whole or any part of said real property to ....James Jones...........
(Buyer's Name)

☒ at a proposed price of $.....200,000.0....

☐ borrow the sum of $............................ at interest of ....%, per annum, for a term of .... *months/years* for the following purposes:
(*If the fiduciary has entered into a contract to sell, attach a copy to application as an exhibit, Schedule "B.")*

THE FIDUCIARY FURTHER REPRESENTS that:

☒ the sale or mortgage of the whole or any part of said real property ☐ is ☒ Y is *not* prohibited by the will or trust instrument.

☐ the real property described in Schedule "A" is not specifically devised.

[X] the real property described in Schedule "A" is specifically devised to ......Jane E. Smith......................
whose written consent to such sale or mortgage is endorsed below.

[X] the fiduciary [ ] *has* [X] *has not* a potential conflict of interest in such sale or mortgage whether as applicant or otherwise.

WHEREFORE THE FIDUCIARY PETITIONS the court praying

[X] for authority to sell and convey the whole or any part of the real property described in Schedule "A"

at [X] *private* [ ] *public* sale.

[ ] for authority to execute a note for said sum of $.............................., to bear interest at the rate of ....%
per annum, for a term of .... *months/years*, and to secure the same by executing a mortgage of the whole or any
part of the real property described in Schedule "A."

[ ] to authorize some disinterested person as a committee to sell and convey the whole or any part of the real property
described in Schedule "A," as the subscriber may wish to be the purchaser of same.

[ ] for authority to sell and convey said property to *himself/herself.*

(Signed) .....Jane E. Smith.....................
Fiduciary

SUBSCRIBED AND SWORN TO BEFORE ME		
	DATE	

....
Judge, Asst. Clerk, Notary Public, Comm. of Sup. Court

CONSENT TO SALE OR MORTGAGE

I, a specific devisee of the above real property described in Schedule "A," consent to its sale or mortgage.

SIGNED	WITNESS	DATE
NAME *[Type or Print]*	SIGNATURE	

APPLICATION TO SELL OR MORTGAGE REAL PROPERTY
PC-400

FORM 15

CERTIFICATE OF NOTICE
FOR LAND RECORDS
PC-251   REV. 11/85
(PRC-36)

STATE OF CONNECTICUT
COURT OF PROBATE
[Type or print]

Court of Probate, District of **Fairfield**   District No. **051**

ESTATE OF

John Andrew Smith

DATE OF CERTIFICATE

8-16-92

PLACE WHERE LAST DWELT	
DATE OF DEATH	**Fairfield, CT**
9-1-89	

☒ DIED TESTATE

☐ DIED INTESTATE

FIDUCIARY *[name, address, zip code and telephone number.]*

Jane E. Smith, 16 Silver Road, Fairfield, CT 312-0000

FIDUCIARY'S POSITION OF TRUST

Executor

DATE OF APPOINTMENT

9-16-89

This certificate is made and caused to be recorded in the land records of the town wherein the said deceased was the owner of real property or any interest therein, or a mortgage or lien upon real property.

(Signed) **Jane E. Smith** . . . .
Fiduciary

CERTIFICATE OF NOTICE FOR LAND RECORDS
PC-251

Appendix B

CONNECTICUT SUCCESSION TAX TABLE
(INCLUDES SURTAX)

EXEMPTIONS BELOW ARE APPLICABLE TO ESTATES OF DECEDENTS DYING ON OR AFTER JULY 1, 1988

RATES AND EXEMPTIONS under the Connecticut Succession Tax are computed according to the class beneficiary and are applied separately to the total value of transfers passing to each class. Transfers to certain charitable organizations or to governmental or government-related organizations are exempt from the Connecticut Succession Tax. (Sec. 12-347 of C.G.S.)

CLASS AA. Spouse

MARITAL DEDUCTION

The marital deduction effectively eliminates a tax on transfers to a spouse. The total marital deduction allowed will be applied by the Commissioner at the time of computation and shown on the assessment. It will include all assets passing to a spouse.

These assets are a part of the gross taxable estate, and must be reported on the appropriate tax schedule. NOTE: Where the gross taxable estate exceeds one million dollars ($1,000,000), but it appears no tax will be due because of the marital exemption for spousal transfers, please file Form S-1 rather than Form S-2.

continued

(Appendix B continues)

CLASS A. Parent; grandparent; adoptive parent; and any natural or adopted descendant. For example: Daughter, son, grandchild, great-grandchild.

(Total Exemption for Class $50,000; included in Table)

IF NET TAXABLE AMOUNT passing to this class is between		Base Amount	THE TAX IS	
			+ %	of excess over
$ 0 -	50,000	$ 0	- -	- -
50,000 -	150,000	0	+ 4.29%	$ 50,000
150,000 -	250,000	4,290	+ 5.72%	150,000
250,000 -	400,000	10,010	+ 7.15%	250,000
400,000 -	600,000	20,735	+ 8.58%	400,000
600,000 -	1,000,000	37,895	+ 10.01%	600,000
Over $1,000,000		77,935	+ 11.44%	1,000,000

CLASS B. Brother or sister (full or half); any natural or adopted descendant of such brother or sister (niece or nephew related by blood); stepchild; son-in-law; daughter-in-law; spouse or unremarried widow(er) of natural or adopted child.

(Total Exemption for Class $6,000; included in Table)

IF NET TAXABLE AMOUNT passing to this class is between		THE TAX IS		
	Base Amount	+ %	of excess over	
$ 0 - 6,000	$ 0	+ – –	– –	
6,000 - 25,000	0	+ 5.72%	$ 6,000	
25,000 - 150,000	1,086.80	+ 7.15%	25,000	
150,000 - 250,000	10,024.30	+ 8.58%	150,000	
250,000 - 400,000	18,604.30	+ 10.01%	250,000	
400,000 - 600,000	33,619.30	+ 11.44%	400,000	
600,000 - 1,000,000	56,499.30	+ 12.87%	600,000	
Over 1,000,000	107,979.30	+ 14.30%	1,000,000	

continued

(Appendix B continues)

CLASS C. All other persons, associations, or corporations not mentioned in Class AA, A, or B. For example: cousin, uncle, aunt, sister-in-law, brother-in-law, step-brother, step-sister, step-grandchild.

(Total Exemption for Class $1,000; included in Table)

IF NET TAXABLE AMOUNT passing to this class is between		THE TAX IS		
		Base Amount	+ %	of excess over
$ 0 -	1,000	$ 0	- -	- -
1,000 -	25,000	0	+ 11.44%	$ 1,000
25,000 -	150,000	2,745.60	+ 12.87%	25,000
150,000 -	250,000	18,833.10	+ 14.30%	150,000
250,000 -	400,000	33,133.10	+ 15.73%	250,000
400,000 -	600,000	56,728.10	+ 17.16%	400,000
600,000 -	1,000,000	91,048.10	+ 18.59%	600,000
Over 1,000,000		165,408.10	+ 20.02%	1,000,000

EXEMPT. Charitable, literary, scientific, historical, religious and government-related organizations.

CONNECTICUT ESTATE TAX. There is also a Connecticut Estate Tax ordinarily applicable only to estates in which substantial amounts of property are taxable for Federal, but not for Succession Tax purposes. It applies only to those estates wherein a Federal Estate Tax return must be filed. This tax is levied on the transfer of the estate of a deceased Connecticut resident and equals the amount by which the maximum credit for state death taxes allowable against the Federal Estate Tax exceeds the aggregate amount of all death taxes paid to Connecticut and all other states. The Connecticut Estate Tax Return is available from the Commissioner of Revenue Services. The tax must be paid within six months and the return must be filed within nine months after the decedent's death unless extensions of time have been granted as provided by law. The tax due is computed by the Commissioner of Revenue Services. Overdue accounts are subject to an interest charge as provided by Statute.

State of Connecticut — Department of Revenue Services
Form S-1 Instructions

Appendix C

SAMPLE CASH REQUIREMENTS AND DISTRIBUTION MEMORANDUM

I. ASSETS

Nature	Recipient	Market Value	Taxable Portion	
			Connecticut	Federal
A. Guardian Life Insurance	Residuary Estate	$ 10,000	$ 0	$ 10,000
B. Interest in Jones Toy Co.	Residuary Estate	100,000	100,000	100,000
C. Residence at 40 Pheasant Lane, New London, CT	Jane Jones	175,000	175,000	175,000
D. Cash and securities	Residuary Estate	50,000	50,000	50,000
E. Furniture, furnishings and other tangible personal property	Jane Jones	50,000	50,000	50,000
	Total Assets of the Estate	385,000	375,000	385,000
	Other Taxable Assets (Non-Probate)*	40,000	5,000	40,000
	TOTAL TAXABLE ASSETS (GROSS ESTATE)	$425,000	$380,000	$425,000

*Insurance and joint bank account passing to Jane Jones

continued

(Appendix C continues)

II. ESTATE DEBTS AND EXPENSES

A. Funeral Expenses		$ 6,000
B. Appraisals		1,500
C. Taxes:		
1. *Real property taxes*		1,000
2. *Federal Income Tax due on final return*		500 (estimated)
D. Settlement Costs		20,000
E. Estate Liabilities		
1. *Note due Jones Toy Co.*		10,000
2. *Mortgage on home*		25,000
F. Miscellaneous Expenses		6,000
	TOTAL DEBTS AND EXPENSES	$70,000

III. TAXES DUE

A. Approximate Federal Estate Tax	$ -0-
B. Approximate Connecticut Succession Tax	10,000
	$ 10,000

IV. CASH REQUIREMENTS

A. Federal Estate Tax	$ -0-
B. Connecticut Succession Tax	10,000
C. Estate Debts and Expenses	70,000
TOTAL CASH REQUIREMENTS	$ 80,000

V. AVAILABLE CASH AND LIQUID ASSETS

A. Cash and securities	$ 50,000
B. Guardian Life Insurance	10,000
	$ 60,000
TOTAL AVAILABLE CASH AND LIQUID ASSETS EXECUTOR MUST RAISE ADDITIONAL CASH REQUIREMENTS OF	$ 20,000

continued

(Appendix C continues)

VI. DISPOSITION OF ESTATE

GROSS ESTATE $425,000

A. Assets Passing outside of Will:
    1. *Insurance and Joint Bank Account* $ 40,000.

B. Assets Passing under Will:
    1. *Tangible personal property passing to Mrs. Jones under Article FOURTH*   50,000.
    2. *New London residence passing to Mrs. Jones under Article SIXTH (I)*   175,000.
    3. *Property passing to Mrs. Jones under Article SIXTH (II)*   80,000.

C. Taxes, Debts and Expenses:
    1. *Federal Estate Tax*   -0-
    2. *Connecticut Succession Tax*   10,000.
    3. *Debts and Expenses*   70,000. $425,000

Appendix D

BIBLIOGRAPHY AND OTHER USEFUL READING MATERIAL FOR THE EXECUTOR

Caine, *Widow* (Morrow, 1974)

Martindale-Hubbell, *Law Dictionary* (R.R. Donnelly & Sons Company, Chicago, Illinois)

Naifeh & Smith, *The Best Lawyers in America* (Seaview, Putnam, New York)

Probate Court Administrator, *Guidelines for Administration of Decedents' Estates* (The Probate Court of Connecticut, Judge Glenn E. Knierim, Probate Court Administrator; 186 Newington Road, West Hartford, Connecticut 06110)

Wilhelm, *The Connecticut Living Trust – Cornerstone of Modern Estate Planning* (Chase Publishing Company, Box 303, Old Greenwich, Connecticut 06870) 1993

Wilhelm, *Connecticut Estates Practice, Death Taxes* (Lawyers Cooperative Publishing Company, Rochester, New York) Second Edition 1984

Wilhelm, *Connecticut Estates Practice, Settlement of Estates* (Lawyers Cooperative Publishing Company, Rochester, New York) Second Edition 1993

Appendix E

FEDERAL ESTATE
AND GIFT TAX RATES[1]

Taxable Estate	Tax[2]	Percent on Excess
$ 600,000	-0-	37%
750,000	$ 55,500	39%
1,000,000	153,000	41%
1,250,000	255,500	43%
1,500,000	363,000	45%
2,000,000	588,000	49%
2,500,000	833,000	53%
3,000,000	1,098,000	55%

[1] Tax rates and exemptions will vary from year to year; the schedule above reflects federal law as of 1993.
[2] Tax after unified credit before state death tax credit.

Appendix F

DISTRIBUTION OF PROPERTY ACCORDING TO CONNECTICUT LAWS OF INTESTACY

Survivors	*Distribution*
Spouse only	Spouse takes all property.
Spouse and descendants (children, grandchildren, etc.)	(1) If all of the decedent's descendants are issue of spouse – spouse takes $100,000 and one-half of the remainder; the descendants take the other one-half of the remainder (*per stirpes*)
	(2) If one or more of decedent's issue are not issue of the spouse – spouse takes one-half of all property; the descendants take one-half of all property (*per stirpes*)
Spouse and parents or parent, but no descendants	Spouse takes $100,000 and three-fourths of the remainder of all property; parent or parents take the other one-quarter
Descendants, but no spouse	All property goes to the descendants (*per stirpes*)
Parents or parent but neither spouse nor descendants	All property goes to the parents or parent
Whole brothers and sisters only	All property goes to decedent's whole brothers and sisters (*per stirpes*); if there are no whole brothers and sisters (or their issue), then the property passes to decedent's half brothers and sisters (*per stirpes*)
None of the above	All property goes to the next of kin in equal degree, kindred of the whole blood taking in preference to kin of the half blood

Appendix G

SAMPLE PROBATE COURT ACCOUNTING

TO THE COURT OF PROBATE FOR THE DISTRICT OF BRIDGEPORT:

ESTATE OF WILLIAM K. SMITH, late of Bridgeport, in said District, deceased.

MARGARET K. SMITH, Executor of the Will of said decedent, hereby exhibits her first and final account from September 17, 1992, the date of her appointment as Executor, to May 4, 1993, to this Court for allowance, to wit:

MARGARET K. SMITH,

Executor

In account with the

ESTATE OF WILLIAM K. SMITH, Deceased

ACCOUNT

DR.

Property on hand, as per Inventory on file in this Court	$85,554.33
Additional assets received after filing of Inventory, as per Schedule A hereof	413.00
Income received, as per Schedule B hereof	1,601.04
Net gain on sale of Estate asset, as per Schedule C hereof	700.00
	$88,268.37

CR.

Funeral expenses and debts of the decedent, as per Schedule D hereof	$ 6,805.95
Administration expenses, as per Schedule E hereof	10,058.08
Distributions of property, as per Schedule F hereof	71,404.34
	$88,268.37

CASH ACCOUNT

DR.

Cash on hand, as per Inventory on file in this Court	$21,519.33
Additional cash, as per Schedule A hereof	413.00
Income received, as per Schedule B hereof	1,601.04
Proceeds on sale of Estate asset, as per Schedule C hereof	60,000.00
	$83,553.37

CR.

Funeral expenses and debts of the decedent, as per Schedule D hereof	$ 6,805.95
Administration expenses, as per Schedule E hereof	10,058.08
Distribution of cash, as per Schedule F hereof	66,669.34
	$83,533.37

Schedule A

Additional Assets Received

Cash balance savings account #4123840, CBT $ 413.00

Schedule B

Income Received

INTEREST:

Connecticut Trust Co., Estate
Savings Account #3200542806

November 26, 1992 $807.38
January 1, 1993   542.37
April 1, 1993   251.29

                                              $ 1,601.04

Schedule C
Net Gain on Sale of Estate Asset

	Proceeds	Cost or Inventory Value	Gain
REAL ESTATE:			
Real property located at 400 River Street, Bridgeport, CT	$60,000.	59,300.	
NET GAIN			$700.

Schedule D

Funeral Expenses and Debts of the Decedent

Funeral Expenses:

7/7/92	St. John's Cemetery		$ 283.00
7/13/92	Miller Funeral Home		2,807.62
10/18/92	Paul's Catering Service		580.00
			$3,670.62

Debts of the Decedent:

7/16/92	City of Bridgeport—Tax Collector, Real Estate			728.99
7/17/92	Shell Oil Credit Card			304.79
7/17/92	SNET			76.06
8/4/92	United Illuminating			163.42
10/15/92	Citytrust Mastercard			1,244.41
10/31/92	City of Bridgeport, Ambulance Service		$49.00	
	Less Medicare reimbursement		(39.20)	9.80
	City of Bridgeport—Tax Collector			
	Real Estate			457.98
	Personal Property			149.88
				3,135.33
				$6,805.95

Schedule E
Administration Expenses

10/18/92	Post Publishing Co., notice to creditors		$ 19.60
	Covenant Group, Homeowners Insurance Policy		
10/18/92	Premium of 10/23/82–83	$ 128.99	
1/2/92	Balance	86.01	215.00
12/22/92	Fairfield County Estate Liquidators, appraisal of tangible personal property		155.25
1/7/93	Realty Co., Peter Johnson, appraisal of real estate		125.00
	Commissioner of Revenue Services,		
4/4/93	Connecticut succession tax	936.21	
	Refund	(9.66)	926.55
4/15/93	Court of Probate, City of Bridgeport, probate fees		357.00
4/4/93	City of Bridgeport, Transfer tax and recording fees		81.00
	Jones & White,		
4/21/93	Legal and accounting fees in connection with administration of Estate	6,000.00	
	Disbursements	78.68	
	Estimated additional disbursements	100.00	6,178.68
	Margaret K. Smith, Executor's fees		2,000.00
			$10,058.08

Schedule F
Distributions of Property
Pursuant to the Decedent's Will

To MARGARET K. SMITH,
  Pursuant to Article Second
    Automobile $ 3,110.00
  Pursuant to Article Third
    4/15/93 Partial distribution   20,000.00
    5/ 4/93   2,531.97
    Tangible personal property   541.66

To PATRICIA SMITH JONES,
  Pursuant to Article Third
    4/15/93 Partial distribution   20,000.00
    5/ 4/93 $2,531.96
                                          (463.27)   2,068.69*
    Tangible personal property   541.67

To JOAN SMITH HAMPTON,
  Pursuant to Article Third
    4/15/93 Partial distribution   20,000.00
    5/ 4/93   2,531.96
                                          (463.28)   2,068.68*
    Tangible personal property   541.67
                                                            $71,404.34

*Beneficiary contributed Connecticut succession tax in amount shown, per Information Schedule I hereof

Information Schedule I
Proration of Connecticut Succession Tax Due

	Amount Passing To Class	Tax on Class	
Net Taxable Estate			$71,617.97
To: MARGARET K. SMITH: Class AA	$26,203.32	-0-	
To: PATRICIA SMITH JONES: Class A	22,707.32	$463.08 .19*	$463.27
To: JOAN SMITH HAMPTON: Class A	22,707.33	$463.09 .19*	463.28
	$71,617.97		$926.55

*Interest

MARGARET K. SMITH, Executor of the Will of WILLIAM K. SMITH, late of Bridgeport, Connecticut, deceased, hereby declares under oath that the foregoing account and the several items thereof are true, and the same is a true statement of all moneys received and expended by her as such Executor during the period of this account, that all claims presented to her have been paid in full and that to the knowledge of said Executor there are no claims or taxes now outstanding.

_____
Margaret K. Smith
Executor

STATE OF CONNECTICUT)
) ss:
COUNTY OF FAIRFIELD)

Subscribed and sworn to by MARGARET K. SMITH, before me, this 8th day of June, 1993

_____
Notary Public

Appendix H

GLOSSARY OF
LEGAL TERMINOLOGY

Accounting A list of all trust transactions filed with the probate court by the executor or administrator after the estate is settled.

Administrator or Administratrix A person or bank selected by the court to settle the estate when the decedent has not named an executor in the will.

Affidavit A written statement made under oath before an officer of the court or a notary public.

Alternative Valuation Date The date six months after death, which under federal tax law, may be used, if desired, rather than the date of decedent's death as the basis for computing estate taxes.

Avoiding probate Arranging your affairs so that at death there is no property to pass under your will and be subject to probate court supervision.

Beneficiary A person who is entitled to share in the estate.

Bequest Personal property or cash left to a beneficiary in a will.

Bond A written promise by an executor or administrator guaranteeing faithful performance of his or her duties. Usually also requires a surety, i.e., another person of financial means (sometimes an insurance company) who guarantees the fiduciary will do the job well and agrees to pay any proven claims against the fiduciary for breach of duty.

Certificate of Devise and Descent A description of real estate passing under the will filed by the executor on the town's land records to show passing of title from the decedent to the beneficiary.

Codicil A legal document adding to or amending a will.

Conservator of the Estate A person or bank appointed by the probate court to manage the property of an incapable person. Occasionally the probate court also may appoint someone, who is known as the conservator of the person, to take personal charge of an incapable person.

Custodian A bank or person who has custody (possession) of trust assets for safekeeping and administrative purposes. Also, a custodian under the *Uniform Gifts to Minors Act* is a person who has temporary control and possession of property for a minor while under age.

Decedent A person who has died and whose estate is being settled.

Deed A written legal document by which title to property (usually real estate) changes hands.

Devise Real estate left in a will to a beneficiary, the devisee. Compare *Legacy*.

Domicile The legal residence of a person; the person's home. Usually determines where the person's will must be probated and state taxes paid.

Donee Person receiving a gift.

Donor Person making a gift.

Estate The property owned by the decedent which is now being managed by the executor or administrator.

Estate Tax (Connecticut) A portion of the federal estate tax collected instead by the State of Connecticut on some estates.

Estate Tax (federal) A graduated tax paid to the federal government based on the value of the estate.

Executor or Executrix The person or bank named by the decedent to settle the estate after death.

Federal Estate Tax Return A tax return filed with the Internal Revenue Service reporting estate assets and deductions. Forms are available at local IRS offices. Also called Form 706.

Fiduciary A person who holds a position of trust, usually involving managing the property of another. Executors, trustees, guardians and conservators are examples.

Fiduciary Income Tax Return The form used to report the estate's annual income tax. Also called Form 1041 (federal) or CT-1041 (Connecticut).

Fiduciary's Certificate A certificate issued by the probate court to an executor or administrator, evidencing the authority of the executor or administrator to act on behalf of the estate.

Fixtures Personal property which is permanently attached to real estate (e.g. plumbing fixtures) and considered to be a part of it.

Flower Bonds Certain issues of government bonds which can be used to pay federal estate taxes on a favorable basis.

Guardian A guardian of the person is responsible for the supervision and control of a minor child; a guardian of the property is responsible for the safekeeping and financial management of the child's assets; a guardian *ad litem* is responsible for representing a minor, an incompetent, or an unascertained person's interests in a particular legal proceeding.

Health Care Proxy A legal document appointing another person to make health care decisions for you.

Hearing A probate court proceeding at which matters involving an estate or trust are discussed before the judge and decisions made.

Heirs or Heirs-at-Law Those person(s) who receive the decedent's estate if there is no will or if the will is not valid.

Intangibles or Intangible Personal Property Property other than real estate which has no intrinsic value, but only represents value. Contrast stock in General Motors (represents value of company's assets) with an actual automobile.

Inter Vivos Trust A trust created during a person's lifetime, as opposed to a trust created by a will. See *Testamentary Trust*; compare *Living Trust*.

Intestate Dying without a will or without a valid will; a person who has died without a will. See *Testator*.

Inventory A list of all estate assets and their values at the decedent's date of death, which is filed with the probate court.

Joint Ownership An arrangement by which two or more persons own property in common. May be with survivorship, in which case a person who dies forfeits all rights to the surviving joint tenant(s); or may be a tenancy-in-common, in which case a deceased joint owner can pass on his or her rights by will.

Jurisdiction The right of a court or taxing authority to control a particular subject matter; e.g., the probate court for the district where a decedent resided has jurisdiction over settlement of his or her estate.

Legacy A bequest under the will other than real estate.

Living Trust A trust created during lifetime, usually revocable, to manage your assets; frequently used to avoid probate.

Living Will A document (not always legally enforceable), stating an individual's wishes with respect to prolonging life during terminal illness.

Marital Deduction For purposes of the federal estate and gift tax, gifts to a spouse are deductible - i.e., not subject to tax.

Nominee Name A brokerage firm or a bank may register title to securities in the name of its agent (nominee) rather than in the name of the executor or administrator to facilitate purchases and sales without the actual signature of the executor or administrator; also known as holding securities in street name.

Non-Claim Statute A state law requiring creditors to file claims against the estate within the period set by the probate court.

Non-Probate Estate Generally, property which the decedent controlled or had an interest in during lifetime, but which was not owned in his or her individual name and, therefore, does not pass through probate. Also includes contractual rights, such as pension plans or insurance, where the individual may name someone other than his or her estate to receive the benefit at death.

Notice   Generally, a written communication from the court to persons interested in the estate that a court hearing is to be held on a matter which concerns them.   Sometimes notices addressed to many persons are published in a local newspaper rather than mailed.

Notice to Creditors   A general notice, published in a local newspaper by the court to all creditors of an estate that they should present their claims promptly.

Paralegal   A non-lawyer employed by a law firm to do routine legal and non-legal tasks, usually at lesser cost to the client.

Per Capita   A distribution equally to a person's children, but not to children of a deceased child.   Contrast *Per Stirpes*.

Personal Property   All property except real property, usually divided into two classes, tangible and intangible personal property.

Per Stirpes   A Latin phrase used by lawyers to indicate that an estate distribution is to be made equally to children, but if a child has died, that child's share passes to his or her children rather than to his or her brothers and sisters.   Contrast *Per Capita*.

Post-mortem   Literally, after death. Commonly used as a prefix, e.g., post-mortem tax planning is used to describe tax techniques for reducing income taxes during estate settlement.

Power of Attorney   Authority from one person to another to act on his or her behalf. May be made durable, i.e., will not be cancelled by incompetency.   Powers of attorney almost always are ended by death.

Probate   Specifically, the legal process by which a will is determined to be valid.   More generally, the entire proceedings by which the estate is managed, taxes and debts paid and the property distributed.

Probate Court   The court in Connecticut which has authority over the settlement of estates.

Probate Estate   The property owned by the decedent which passes under the will and is managed by the executor or administrator.

Probate Judge An elected official who presides over the probate court.

Real Property Real estate, including various interests in real estate such as mineral rights.

Refunding Agreement An agreement by a beneficiary who has received estate assets that he or she will refund them if needed to pay estate obligations.

Residuary Estate What is left in the estate for distribution after payment of all debts, taxes, administration expenses, bequests and devises.

Return of Claims A list of all claims filed against the estate, which is filed by the executor or administrator with the probate court.

Revocable Trust A trust which can be cancelled at any time by the person who established it.

Right of Election A surviving spouse's statutory right to forego any benefits under the will and instead have set aside for him or her a share of the estate. In Connecticut, the share consists of a lifetime interest in one-third of the spouse's probate estate.

Statutory Share The portion of an estate which a surviving spouse has a statutory right to have set aside in trust for his or her lifetime. See *Right of Election.*

Succession Tax A graduated inheritance tax paid to Connecticut, based on the value of the inheritance of each beneficiary and the degree of kinship of the beneficiary to the decedent.

Succession Tax Return The Connecticut inheritance tax return. Also called Form S-1.

Tangibles or Tangible Personal Property Property other than real estate which has intrinsic value (automobiles, household goods, clothing, jewelry, etc.). Contrast with stock certificates, money, etc., which only represent value and are termed intangibles.

Taxable Estate Property which is subject to estate or inheritance tax because of the decedent's death, regardless of whether the decedent owned the property or whether the property passes through probate.

Tax Waivers Written permission from the taxing authorities waiving their right to collect taxes on property which the executor decides to sell. Potential buyers must be wary of purchasing estate property subject to taxes without a tax waiver, because the tax may be collected from the buyer if not paid by the seller.

Testamentary Trust A trust which is created by a will. Compare *Inter Vivos Trust*.

Testate A person who dies and leaves a valid will is said to have died testate. Compare *Intestate*.

Testator or Testatrix A person who makes a will.

Totten Trust A revocable trust bank account.

Trust A three-party arrangement for management and distribution of property; usually involves a grantor or testator (who creates the trust and contributes the property), a trustee (who manages the property), and one or more beneficiaries (the person[s] for whose benefit the trust is to be managed). A trust may be created by a will or by lifetime agreement. It is usually written; its terms spell out how the property is to be managed and distributed.

Unified Credit The basic tax credit available to offset the first part of the federal estate tax otherwise due from each estate. Also can be used during lifetime to offset the first part of the gift tax.

Widow's or Widower's Allowance A sum which can be paid from the estate if ordered by the court for support of the surviving spouse for a reasonable period of time.

CHASE PUBLISHING COMPANY
Post Office Box 303EH
Old Greenwich, Connecticut 06870

PLEASE SEND ME:

____copies *The Connecticut Living Trust* @ $14.95 $_____

____copies *The Executor's Handbook –* @ $14.95 $_____
            A Practical Guide to Settling
            Estates, Second Edition

6% Sales tax per book (Conn. residents only) $_____

Shipping and handling:
    For 1 book - add $2.40; 2 books - add $3.52;
    3 or more books - add 10% $_____
TOTAL ENCLOSED: $_____
Make checks payable to Chase Publishing Company.

SHIP BOOKS TO: *(Please print)*

NAME_____PHONE_____

STREET_____

CITY/TOWN_____STATE____ZIP_____

- -

CHASE PUBLISHING COMPANY
Post Office Box 303EH
Old Greenwich, Connecticut 06870

PLEASE SEND ME:

____copies *The Connecticut Living Trust* @ $14.95 $_____

____copies *The Executor's Handbook –* @ $14.95 $_____
            A Practical Guide to Settling
            Estates, Second Edition

6% Sales tax per book (Conn. residents only) $_____

Shipping and handling:
    For 1 book - add $2.40; 2 books - add $3.52;
    3 or more books - add 10% $_____
TOTAL ENCLOSED: $_____
Make checks payable to Chase Publishing Company.

SHIP BOOKS TO: *(Please print)*

NAME_____PHONE_____

STREET_____

CITY/TOWN_____STATE____ZIP_____